Free Small Group Videos

Seven short videos (Average length 12 minutes)

~ Reading the book is like studying the blueprints of a house.
~ Watching the seven videos is like walking through the house.

In the videos you will pray on each piece of armor.
You will personally experience the power of each weapon.

Three free ways to watch the videos

1. PrayersAnsweredImmediately.org - video series tab

2. YouTube.com - type in: *"Prayers Answered Immediately Playlist"*

3. Scan this QR code with your smart phone to go directly to the YouTube playlist.
   Don't have a QR reader?
   Search "QR code reader" in your phone's app store

Purchasing a DVD of all seven videos

At the PrayersAnsweredImmediatly.org website, under the "Video Series" tab, is an option to purchase the DVD for $10 plus shipping. All seven videos are included on one DVD.

Other Free Resources

At PrayersAnsweredImmediatly.org, the "Free Resources" tab has many free downloads of additional tools to assist in your prayer life.

Prayers Answered Immediately

John Fichtner

Prayers Answered Immediately!

Unless otherwise indicated, Scripture quotations are from THE HOLY BIBLE, NEW INTERNATIONAL VERSION®, NIV® Copyright © 1973, 1978, 1984, 2011 by Biblica, Inc.® Used by permission. All rights reserved worldwide.

Cover Design: Inspired Graphics / inspiredgraphics.net
Published By: PAI Publishing, 2014
Printed in the United States of America
ISBN 978-0-692-26803-2

Table of Contents

1

My Story and Others

My story – 1988

My prayer life stinks! I don't think I know how to pray.

Some days, I am a fragile, shattered mess, and my prayers echo off the wall. Other days, I am embarrassed at how boring I find prayer. Many busy days I skip prayer. What difference does it make anyway? After days without prayer, I am dry and weak. God feels a million miles away.

I have been a Christian for 11 years. I have been a pastor for 7 years. Are my prayers even answered? I am weak and ashamed.

Every now and then, I get so desperately tired that I cry out in deep agony. Sometimes the clouds part, and I connect with Heaven. Other times, Heaven remains closed no matter how many tears I shed. I am bone weary of my prayer life consisting of reactions to crises.

When empty, I run to media or I talk with people. Why can't I run to Jesus when I need to be filled?

It's easy to talk with my wife. Why can't I talk with Jesus that way?
Why is prayer so confusing, so hard, and so impractical?

Those had been my words for 11 years.

Then in 1988, Jesus taught me specific prayers that the Lord answers
immediately. The reason for God's prompt response is because each
of these prayers involves asking God to give us more of his heart in
a Biblical area, directly related to a specific piece of God's armor.

The 7 pieces of armor Biblically represent 7 daily subjects in our
lives of: Conflicts, Emotions, Schedule, Favor, Thoughts, Hearing
God's Voice, and Readiness.

Everything changed when I had God's instant reply to my prayers in
practical areas of life. Prayer became fun, fascinating, and easy. My
soul became filled with God's presence and joy.

I've tested this prayer model for over 25 years. The end result is that
my life has been daily changed. I now know, with absolute certainty,
that God answers these prayers. When I pray on God's armor, I
have a day that is 10 times better. This book is my story.

The goal of this book

Paul promised that understanding and applying God's armor can
make you strong in Jesus. When Jesus' strength flows through you,
everything in life is easier, you win victories, and you fulfill God's
purposes in your life. Your soul is healthy, and you are alive and
vibrant spiritually because prayer is delightful and productive.

Be strong in the Lord and in his mighty power. Ephesians 6:10

With this potential, I ask you to approach this book as a map to a
treasure. I ask you to prioritize 10-15 minutes daily to study this
book and underline key sentences. After you have studied the book
and watched the free YouTube videos, I earnestly ask you to put
your entire heart into the ten day test.

4 unique aspects of this book

1. <u>The Videos!</u>
   This book is like studying a blueprint for a beautiful house.
   The videos are like touring that house. In the videos, you see me
   pray on each piece of armor. You will personally experience the
   power of each weapon. The 7 free videos have an average length
   of approximately 12 minutes each. They can be used in a small
   group setting or in your personal study.

2. <u>The 10 Day Test!</u>
   This is a simple concept. After you finish the book and videos,
   tear out one of the prayer sheets at the back of the book to pray
   on God's armor for 7 days. Then spend 3 days praying any way
   you want, except that you do not pray on God's armor. The
   impact of the ten day test is in the contrast. For 7 days you will
   experience God in greater depth. In those 3 "armor-less" days
   you get a clear comparison between other prayers and the power
   of praying on God's armor.

3. <u>The Stories!</u>
   In 1994, I began to share these 7 pieces of armor with my
   church family. In each section of the book, I have stories from
   individuals related to that specific piece of armor.

4. <u>The Special Offer to Pastors!</u>
   I have dedicated 100% of the profits from this book to
   supporting pastors. Praying on God's armor can transform an
   entire church. Appendix C explains this offer in detail.

Skip the rest of this chapter

The rest of this chapter contains four general stories of lives that
have been changed through praying on God's armor. Personally, I
like to skim a book quickly and get to the meat of the message. If
you are like me, then you may want to jump ahead to the second

chapter. My wife enjoys soaking in a book and loves the big picture warmth of testimonies. If you relate to my wife, then soak on!

Joe

Joe pastors a church on the east side of town. He is a faithful man in his 50s with a small congregation of 175 people. Joe loves Jesus and his people. However, he has always had a secret fear that has kept him up at night. He hasn't been sure that he knew how to walk out this Christian life. Here are Joe's own words.

Hey John,

I have to tell you what has happened to me. For years, I have read Bible verses, books, commentaries, testimonies, and Internet articles that make it very clear that a person cannot live the Christian life in his own power. The Lord Jesus Christ has to live it through him.

I wholeheartedly agree with this and embrace it as absolute truth. But I did NOT KNOW HOW this was transacted. I told Jesus that I would give anything to get out of the way and to let him live his life through me. I have determined over and over, by faith, to believe that this is happening, but I kept running into me.

Then I learned to pray on God's armor. Now, I understand! After so many years, I now know that Jesus hears my prayers. Even more, I now feel him guiding me and living his life through me. I am actually becoming confident. I cannot thank you enough for teaching me that prayer is practical.

Joe

Spencer and Crystal

Spencer and Crystal were new visitors who came to me with their marriage on the rocks. They were discussing divorce. The root issue was that they were both spiritually dry. They had been Christians for over 20 years, but their prayer lives were dull and erratic.

After praying on God's armor for a few weeks, every area of their marriage turned around. Here is Crystal's email.

Hello Pastor John,

Praying on God armor every day has been life-changing. I am just so amazed at how my days progress. After praying on each piece of the armor I notice many things:

- *I am very productive.*

- *My thoughts are much more clear and focused.*

- *I have a sense of peace, joy, and confidence.*

- *God answers many of my questions and prayers.*

- *I continue to feel an excitement and hunger to read his word.*

- *I find myself praying for others and thinking of ways I can be a blessing to them.*

God has really been showing me how to stay focused in my life. He is especially revealing things to me about each one of my children.

I'm definitely praying for them more and wanting to share the word of God with them so they will know how to lean on him for the trials they experience in their lives.

Even more amazing is what I am seeing in my husband. He is excited about his prayer life. We have been married for over 20 years, and we have been Christians even longer. I have never seen him excited about prayer until now.

Thank you so much!

Crystal

Crystal's husband, Spencer, sent me his first email later that month.

Hi Pastor John,

I now find it exciting to pray in the mornings for several reasons. I pray out loud in the car on the way to work, and I feel that the conversation with my heavenly Father is growing stronger. I've noticed things more clearly than ever. I feel strong. I feel ready for the day. The best part is that it lasts all day. I don't crash in the evenings like I used to do. I want to pray on God's armor for the rest of my life.

Spencer

Spencer's second email, sent a few weeks later, had a profound insight. Spencer discovered why the 10 day test ends with 3 days of not praying on the armor.

Hi Pastor John,

I want to tell you about last week. I had 2 days in a row where I did not pray on the armor. I thought that it was just because I was so busy. Honestly, though, I think I wanted to see what would happen if I skipped a day or two.

On the first day, I felt weak and confused about things, but I just kept plugging. By the end of the day, I was pretty rattled. Even so, I skipped prayer time the next day. I just pretended that I was going to try to talk to God all day, like I used to do.

By the second day, I knew that the opposite of being strong is being weak. I overreacted to lots of things. I made many stupid decisions. I was frustrated and empty. A week later, I am still trying to fix the things I messed up in those 2 days.

The next day, I couldn't wait to pray on God's armor. It was so refreshing. I could feel God being pleased with me again. I was calm and peaceful. I had God's wisdom and favor all day. I have prayed on God's armor every day since then.

A month ago, I told you that I "wanted" to pray on God's armor for the rest of my life. Now I "know" that I will pray on God's armor for the rest of my life.

I like being strong in Jesus, and I really hate being weak, empty, and frustrated.

I will forever be grateful that you showed me that prayer can be practical, simple, and powerful!

Spencer

After this second email I knew I had a "lifer." Years later, this couple is still doing fantastic and praying on God's armor daily.

I have seen over 3,000 people's lives changed in our church through this practical prayer. Once they become comfortable praying on God's armor, they pray it almost every day for the rest of their lives.

The Bible says that God' armor can make you strong. When you are strong, life is easier, you in more victories, and you fulfill God's purposes in your life.

Be strong in the Lord and in his migh power. Ephesians 6:10

Pete

Hi Pastor John,

Below is my testimony of how your book changed my life.

In April of 2010, I found myself in the midst of a difficult crisis. My marriag of 15 years to my wife, Betty, was falling apart. No matter how hard I tried in the flesh, there was nothing I could do to save it. My marriage, family, home, and finances were literally thrown into chaos.

I had been a Christian for years, and I had been doing all the stuff I thought I was supposed to do. I was faithful to tithe, attend church, and serve in leadership roles when called upon. While it looked like I was doing everything right by outward appearance, in reality, my behavior and actions did not always reflect Christ. In fact, sometimes it was probably hard to tell if I was even a Christian. My actions reflected the reality that I was in charge of my life, and I only let Christ in when I needed his help. Spending time with God in prayer was not a priority. I was just too busy.

There is a scripture verse (Jeremiah 17:9) that says the heart is deceitful above all things. Scripture also says God is no respecter of persons (Acts 10:34) but judges by what is in your heart (1 Sam 16:7).

Let's be blunt! No one is anxious to face painful realities or examine their own shortcomings. Neither was I.

I went to see my pastor, John, for advice. PJ was a mentor and friend I trusted, who loved me enough to tell me the truth. He challenged me to be honest with myself and with God. For the first time in my life, I was forced to really examine my heart and the fruits of living for myself. Once I did, I could clearly see how wretched and full of self I was.

PJ gave me one strategy. Pray, every day, for one hour. He even offered to teach me how. I had always prayed, but it was never for more than a couple of minutes a day. Praying for an hour seemed impossible, a mountain I could never climb.

After I understood the armor, it became easier and actually enjoyable. I felt the peace of God come over me. After a week, I found myself waking up with a yearning to pray, and I was sad when the hour was over. Prayer time became the highlight of my day. I also started memorizing chapters of the Bible.

Although I prayed fervently for healing and reconciliation in my marriage, Betty and I did eventually divorce in 2011. Through it all, I continued to put on God's armor, quote the word, and pray.

But then, in the ashes of that dead marriage, something amazing happened. Betty started praying as well. Both of us turned our hearts deeper into Jesus.

Two years later, in May of 2013, Betty and I remarried. I think we would both agree and say the second time around is WAY better than the first! Our marriage is proof that NOTHING is impossible with God.

I have now memorized 7 chapters of God's word, and I still average an hour a day with the Lord. Putting the Armor of God on me and my family is a daily priority now. I do it every day on my drive to work.

When I do, we walk in confidence, my schedule seems manageable, and there is harmony in my home. On the days when I forget to or fail to put on the armor, inevitably there is confusion and things do not seem to go as well.

Thank you, John, for showing me how to pray with power, authority, and purpose!

Your pal,
Pete

Katrina – has prayed on the armor for 20 years

Pastor John,

Since 1994, I have implemented praying on the Armor of God, out loud, after you shared your deep revelation on the detailed effectiveness of each piece of armor. It has transformed my prayer life and my soul. Once I understood each piece, I was able to understand where my life needed focus each day. I learned what a high value the Lord has placed on my being protected from the enemy.

I also prayed it with my children, aloud, on the way to school. It gave me insights into how they were feeling and what their struggles were that day.

We personalized the image of the shoes for me to know how they felt about their day, such as, running shoes, hiking boots, ballet shoes, house slippers. It was a fun way to experiment of adjusting to children.

Any structure that is still effective after 20 years is definitely from God, and I am certain it will change many people's lives, like it did mine. It has been so easy and yet so profound. Now, I run out of time instead of not praying or having short prayers.

You rock PJ! I know I don't always take enough time to thank you for allowing the Lord to use you in transforming my life, and many others, with your revelation of the Scriptures. I share with people all the time the precepts I have gained from your teaching. I am thankful the Lord led us to Liberty and that we are still growing 20 years later.

Katrina

Ephesians 6:10-18

Finally, be strong in the Lord and in his mighty power. [11] Put on the full armor of God, so that you can take your stand against the devil's schemes. [12] For our struggle is not against flesh and blood, but against the rulers, against the authorities, against the powers of this dark world and against the spiritual forces of evil in the heavenly realms. [13] Therefore put on the full armor of God, so that when the day of evil comes, you may be able to stand your ground, and after you have done everything, to stand.

1. **Conflicts**
   [14] Stand firm then, with the belt of truth buckled around your waist

2. **Emotions**
   with the breastplate of righteousness in place

3. **Schedule**
   [15] and with your feet fitted with the readiness that comes from the gospel of peace.

4. **Favor**
   [16] In addition to all this, take up the shield of faith, with which you can extinguish all the flaming arrows of the evil one.

5. **Thoughts**
   [17] Take the helmet of salvation

6. **God's voice**
   and the sword of the Spirit, which is the word of God.

7. **Ready**
   [18] And pray in the Spirit on all occasions with all kinds of prayers and requests. With this in mind, be alert and always keep on praying for all the Lord's people.

Conflicts
=
Belt of Truth

2

Humility – I Am "Right" but I Don't Have Truth

Conflict is Satan's greatest weapon.

The purpose of the Armor of God is to protect us from the attacks of Satan.

The ugliest, deepest, and most painful wounds ever inflicted in our lives have come through conflicts. Through our spouses, parents, children, co-workers, or friends, Satan has pierced our soul. We play back the strife-filled memories like endless loops of a grisly horror film. We relive the anger, accusations, high-volume, and excessive agony.

Our society is becoming more dysfunctional. Families are fractured. Homes are no longer safe. In this war zone, living with the infected, festering wounds of contention has become the expected way of life.

I see the daily devastation of dissension. Like most pastors, I've found that conflict resolution accounts for 90% of my counseling.

The purpose of the Belt of Truth is to remove and resolve all conflicts in our lives.

The Belt of Truth is the hardest weapon to learn.

You may struggle with the first few chapters. The armor of God deals with the toughest subject first.

> ➤ If you win this battle, the Belt of Truth will give you a strife-free life, and you will find every other piece of armor to be easy and powerful.

> ➤ If you lose this battle for God's truth in conflicts, then Satan will regularly explode dissension into your life in order to steal every other piece of your inheritance.

Please persevere through these first few chapters so you can succeed in every other area of your life.

Humility

Splat! Joey was immediately red faced as he heard the hamburger squish under him.

"Watch out!" Billy said as he shoved Joey.

"Get outta my face!" Joey blurted out as he shoved Billy back. Knocking chairs over, the former friends tumbled to the floor while the crowd quickly gathered.

"Stop! Stop! Stop!" Mrs. Whitaker, their 5th grade teacher, leapt into action. She quickly broke up the tussle before anyone got hurt.

The next day, Billy's mom stormed into the principal's office demanding that Mrs. Whitaker be reprimanded. Over the next week, the tension escalated. Let's survey the situation as we see 10 different perspectives entangled in one small incident.

1. Billy's perspective is that… *"Joey sat on my sandwich. I wasn't hitting him. I was just moving him off my sandwich."*

2. Billy's Mom's perspective is that … *"Mrs. Whitaker should have more control over the cafeteria and should be held responsible."*

3. Billy's Dad's perspective is that … *"Everyone is making too big of a deal about this."*

4. Mrs. Whitaker's perspective is that … *"The issue is funding and the school board should spend more money on extra cafeteria monitors."*

5. Billy's principal's perspective is that … *"Society as a whole has gotten too permissive."*

6. Billy's friend's perspective is that … *"The whole thing was hilarious."*

7. Joey's perspective is that … *"The sandwich shouldn't have been on my chair, and Billy hit me first."*

8. Joey's Mom's perspective is that … *"Billy's mom always thinks Billy is innocent."*

9. Joey's Dad's perspective is that… *"Joey did right in defending himself."*

10. Joey's friend's perspective is that … *"The whole thing was hilarious."* (Since Billy's friend is also Joey's friend, he gets to express his opinion twice! ☺)

Now people are angry. Meetings become shouting matches. How far will this blow-up escalate?

The sad part is that every individual person is accurate in his or her perspective. They all have a small portion of the truth, but none of them have the full truth. If they were humble, then they would recognize that they are "right," but they don't have the "truth."

Biblically, truth resolves conflicts

Three passages in the New Testament deal extensively with the subject of truth. In all 3 of these passages, the background subject is about dealing with strife.

1. In John 8, Jesus was in an intense conflict with the Pharisees. It was in the context of Jesus calling the Pharisees "liars" and "children of the devil" that Jesus spoke the famous words:

    Then you will know the truth, and the truth will set you free. John 8:32

2. Ephesians 4 challenges us to grow up and learn how to resolve tension in a calm, Biblical, gracious manner.

    Speaking the truth in love, we will in all things grow up. Ephesians 4:15

    Later in the same chapter, Paul expands this by dealing with the anger that comes through conflicts. Paul says:

    Therefore each of you must put off falsehood and speak truthfully to his neighbor, for we are all members of one body.
    In your anger do not sin.
    Do not let the sun go down while you are still angry
    and do not give the Devil a foothold. Ephesians 4:25-27

3. In 1 John, we find the word "truth" 11 times in 5 chapters. Constantly intermingled with the subject of truth is the Apostle John's request that Christians resolve their conflicts.

    I am writing you a new command; its truth is seen in him and you, because the darkness is passing and the true light is already shining.
    Anyone who claims to be in the light,
    but hates his brother is still in darkness. 1 John 2:8-9

In putting on the Belt of Truth, we are resolving to deal with all conflicts on the basis of truth!

How do I do this?

With the belt of truth buckled around your waist. Ephesians 6:14

The picture of the belt is a graphic analogy of how truth can resolve conflicts.

Truth begins with understanding every perspective of an issue!

When we put on a belt, we take a single piece of leather, and we wrap it completely around the subject. Some of us have bigger "subjects" than others ☺. As we wrap this belt around the subject, we slowly and methodically weave it through each belt loop.

In a sense, each belt loop represents a small, locked-in viewpoint related to the discussion. Each belt loop has a part of the picture. None of these belt loops see the entire circumference. Like a belt loop, we are attached to our context. We lock into our viewpoint through:

1. The facts we know
2. Our past experiences, wounds, and successes
3. Our motives
4. Our personalities

Jesus, who is truth (John 14:6), sees the entire picture.

Human tension may be the greatest test of how much we love Jesus. This is why the belt comes first in the armor. When the tension of a misunderstanding invades our soul, we have a choice.

➤ We know that our points are valid and our passions are positive. Our flesh screams for our points to be fully appreciated and understood by others.

➤ The pain begins in recognizing that the other person's points and passions are just as valid.

➤ The pain increases when we realize that their legitimate points expose our weaknesses and blind spots.

> ➤ Our flesh wants to fiercely embrace the foolish deception that we see the entire picture.

> ➤ Our flesh wants to demand that everyone focus exclusively on our perspective.

When faced with compelling points on the other side of the Belt of Truth, we want to deny or make excuses. We are just like our great grandparents, Adam and Eve, who blamed each other and tried to cover their nakedness with fig leaves. We come up with feeble "fig leaf" excuses to deny the truth of the other person's perspective and cover our weaknesses.

God's Word commands us to be humble and consider that Jesus may want to teach us something through some area that this irritating person sees more clearly than we do.

We must choose! Do we love our self-righteous stance that our tiny belt loop is all that matters, or do we love Jesus more?

When we love Jesus more, we acknowledge that every single person has some insight that is accurate! It doesn't matter whether their insight is minor or major. What is essential is that we cannot hear Jesus' heart until we search for some point of validity in the other's viewpoint.

Even when we understand every human perspective in a conflict, we might not grasp all of the truth that God wants us to see. However, the Belt of Truth gets us started toward God's truth.

Now, the question is ... "How do we quickly resolve this conflict?" Isn't that the question of a lifetime?

3

Step One -

Please Help Me to Understand Why You…?

My opening words

I am standing at a gas station pumping gas into our family car. My precious family and some of my dearest friends are sitting inside the car.

A moment later, I am handed a fiery torch. I did not ask for this fire. I did not want this flame in my hands. However, I am now responsible for what I do with this combustion.

I glance to my left and discover that I have accidentally spilled some of the gasoline over the side of the car and onto the ground. I glance to my right and see an open bucket of water. What I do in this moment is pivotal. Do I carelessly throw the flame toward the ground? After all, I didn't ask for this inferno.

The fiery torch is our irritation over a misunderstanding. We did not ask for this burning in our hearts. We did not want this fire.

The direction we throw the torch represents our opening words.

We have all seen conflicts that left family and friends burned and scarred. The price tag of careless opening words in a tense dialogue is immense.

Most opening words are a torch thrown toward the gasoline. They quickly escalate the dialogue into an ugly battle.

1. "Why do you always…?"
2. "I need for you to understand that…!"
3. "Didn't I tell you…?"
4. "You really hurt my feelings when you…!"

All four of these lines increase strife, but the worst of them is the last one.

Framed on the wall

Mounted on the wall of our church office is a chart on a standard-sized 8.5 x 11 inch piece of paper in a nice frame. It is hanging directly in front of our copier machine. It gives people something interesting to read while waiting for their papers.

It charts the effects of the worst and best single-line openings.

1. You hurt my feelings when you…!

2. Can you please help me to understand why you…?

The diagram is fascinating, painful, inspiring, and eye-opening.

Vertical reading – what Heaven hears!

Reading the entire left column and then the entire right column in a vertical pattern hammers the impact of our opening words. I like to think of reading these columns in a vertical pattern as a picture of what Heaven hears when we say these words.

Horizontal Reading – what the other person hears!

Reading through this chart, row by row, gives sharp clarity and contrast to the effect of these words on the person receiving them.

What is **communicated** *(What people hear!)* when I open a conversation with the words…	
You HURT my FEELINGS when you…!	**Can you please HELP me to UNDERSTAND why you…?**
I am PERFECT! I see all! I know all! There is no need for dialogue! I know all of your motives and actions, and I have already made my judgments! You are evil! I am the innocent victim, and you must be punished.	**I am FLAWED!** I am sure that there were words or actions that I misunderstood. You may have information that completely changes the picture for me.
I want STRIFE! With my opening words, I have made it clear that we are not allies. We are not teammates. My goal is not compromise. You are an adversary, and I will intentionally escalate this tension. Anger, judging, self-pity, and strife are my goals.	**I want PEACE!** Most misunderstandings will never be fully resolved this side of heaven. Jesus sees so much more than we do. It usually takes me years to sort out everything Jesus is trying to teach me through a misunderstanding. Whether we draw a step closer or wind up a step more distant through this dialogue, I am committed to be kind, gentle, calm, and gracious. *Heb. 12:14 Make every effort to live in peace with all men.* *Rom. 12:18 If it is possible, as far as it depends on you, live at peace with everyone.*
I am here to ATTACK! My emotions are all that I care about. That is why I use the opening line, *"You hurt my FEELINGS!"* I don't care about truth. I don't want dialogue. I don't care what you "think" you may have been trying to do. I command you to sit still while I shred you, judge your motives, and point out how terrible you are.	**I am here to LISTEN** Sometimes my emotions are terrible liars. When I am in pain, my emotions can try to lead me toward evil judgments. Evil emotions are to be crucified with Jesus. Venting gives my evil emotions more power. When I listen well, I often hear something that completely changes my perspective, calms my emotions and fills me with Jesus' love. *Prov. 18:13 To answer before listening - that is folly & shame.* *Ja. 1:19 My dear brothers, take note of this: Everyone should be quick to listen, slow to speak and slow to become angry.*
I want Jesus to be as HARSH with me as I am with you! I am asking Jesus to expose every point of evil in my heart and to judge me without mercy, just like I am doing with you. *Matthew 7:1-2 Do not judge, or you too will be judged. ² For in the same way you judge others, you will be judged, and with the measure you use, it will be measured to you.*	**I want Jesus to give me MERCY!** I have found that – in most misunderstandings – there are assumptions and errors on both sides. My first goal is to find my own errors. For your errors, I want to give mercy so that I may receive mercy. *Matthew 5:7 Blessed are the merciful, for they will be shown mercy.*

You may download a copy of this single page document at PrayersAnsweredImmediately.org under the "Free Resources" tab.

On the following pages, you will find the words from this chart in a larger font size so that it is more readable.

Left side of the chart – damaging, destructive opening words!

What is communicated *(What people hear!)* when I open a conversation with the words…

You HURT my FEELINGS when you...!

I am PERFECT!

I see all! I know all! There is no need for dialogue!

I know all of your motives and actions, and I have already made my judgments! You are evil!

I am the innocent victim, and you must be punished.

I want STRIFE!

With my opening words, I have made it clear that we are not allies. We are not teammates. My goal is not compromise.

You are an adversary, and I will intentionally escalate this tension.

Anger, judging, self-pity, and strife are my goals.

I am here to ATTACK!

My emotions are all that I care about. That is why I used the opening line, "You hurt my FEELINGS!"

I don't care about truth. I don't want dialogue.

I don't care what you "think" you may have been trying to do.

I command you to sit still while I shred you, judge your motives, and point out how terrible you are.

I want Jesus to be as HARSH with me as I am with you!

I am asking Jesus to expose every point of evil in my heart and to judge me without mercy, just like I am doing with you.

Matthew 7:1-2 Do not judge, or you too will be judged. [2] For in the same way you judge others, you will be judged, and with the measure you use, it will be measured to you.

Right side of the chart – humble, dialogue opening words!

Can you please HELP me to UNDERSTAND why you...?

I am FLAWED!

I am sure there were words or actions that I misunderstood. You may have information that completely changes the picture for me.

I want PEACE!

Most misunderstandings will never be fully resolved this side of Heaven. Jesus sees so much more than we do.

It usually takes me years to sort out everything Jesus is trying to teach me through a misunderstanding.

Whether we draw a step closer or wind up a step more distant through this dialogue, I am committed to be kind, gentle, calm and gracious. *Hebrews 12:14 Make every effort to live in peace with all men. Romans 12:18 If it is possible, as far as it depends on you, live at peace with everyone.*

I am here to LISTEN

Sometimes my emotions are terrible liars. When I am in pain, my emotions can try to lead me toward evil judgments. Evil emotions are to be crucified with Jesus.

Venting gives my evil emotions more power.

When I listen well, I often hear something that completely changes my perspective, calms my emotions, and fills me with Jesus' love. *Proverbs 18:13 To answer before listening - that is folly and shame. James 1:19 My dear brothers, take note of this: Everyone should be quick to listen, slow to speak and slow to become angry.*

I want Jesus to give me MERCY!

I have found that – in most misunderstandings – there are assumptions and errors on both sides. My first goal is to find my own errors. For your errors, I want to give mercy so that I may receive mercy. *Matthew 5:7 Blessed are the merciful, for they will be shown mercy.*

What the other person hears!

It is essential to understand the heading of this chart.
What is communicated
(What people hear!)
when I open a conversation with the words…

The left side of this chart is very revealing for those who live in ignorance of the effect of their words. Many people are raised in an environment where powerful curses proceeding from mouths are a normal occurrence.

This chart has the ability to set people free from the destructive words they speak.

As you read the left side of this chart, please understand that I am not saying that all of this was the intent of your heart.

When you said to someone, "You hurt my feelings when you…!" it may not have been your premeditated plan to tell them that you:

> ➢ Think you are perfect,
> ➢ Want strife,
> ➢ Are here to attack, &
> ➢ Are asking Jesus to be as harsh with you as you are being with this other person.

Although it may not have been your calculated intent, this is what they heard, and it is what is heard in Heaven.

Please let Jesus give you understanding of what is heard through your words so that you speak life instead of death into misunderstandings.

The tongue has the power of life and death, and
those who love it will eat its fruit. Proverbs 18:21

Dousing the torch in the bucket of water

In our gas station analogy, to protect your family you must intentionally turn to the right and bend down to place the lit torch in the bucket of water. Because of the danger you would probably inconvenience yourself by submerging your hand in the water to ensure the safety of those you love.

To open a dialogue with the words, "Can you please help me to understand why you...?" requires all of these elements.

You must see the danger, turn away from your fleshly reaction, bend down in humility, and immerse yourself in the water of praying for Jesus's love in order to ensure the safety of those whom you love.

In small, petty situations, the tension never surfaces.

With the opening words, "Can you please help me to understand why you...?" the other person immediately understands that you are trying to move away from tension and earnestly desire peace. You have committed to sincerely listen, and you want them to feel safe.

In many minor, daily irritations, these words instantly put out the fire. When the other person answers your question, their response may surprise you with information you didn't see before.

The husband says, "Babe, can you please help me to understand why you put in two dryer sheets when you dry the clothes?" He is battling irritation at the waste of money. She responds, "My skin is sensitive to static. With one dryer sheet, my clothes still itch all day long. When I use two dryer sheets, the clothes are comfortable, smell good, and make me feel soft and gentle."

He now has a goofy smile on his face, and he realizes that he was being silly and that she had valid logic. A foolish argument was cancelled by him carefully burying the lit torch of irritation in the bucket of water.

To answer before listening, that is folly and shame Proverbs 18:13

Recently, a wife told me about learning the power of this opening line. She and her husband had a history of some loud, dramatic arguments.

They were on their way home with their children when they stopped at a gas station. While the husband was getting the gas, the wife bought a few things, including a bag of potato chips. As they were driving away, the husband told the children not to open the potato chips. A few minutes later, the children opened the chips.

When the husband got upset, the wife was certain she knew why. She was sure her husband was upset because he was a control freak. She thought he was being selfish and mean. What was so wrong about the children having a few potato chips? She was just about to let him have an earful when she remembered the importance of her opening words. She said to him, "Can you please help me to understand why you won't let the kids have some potato chips?"

To her surprise, he responded, "Babe, I don't want them eating now because you said that it bothers you when the kids eat before dinner and then don't want your dinner. I know that you put a great meal in the crock pot earlier for us to eat when we get home, and I want them to appreciate how hard you work for them."

The wife was astounded. She had almost yelled at her husband because she thought he was too harsh with the kids. By choosing a different opening line, she avoided judging her husband and cancelled a major fight.

So many arguments erupt over petty issues. What a wonderful life we can have when we avoid frivolous strife.

This opening line also has a positive effect in large, important misunderstandings.

In major, volatile situations, the tension lessens.

Can you please help me to understand:

> ➢ "Why you felt the need to get angry?"
> ➢ "Why you do drugs?"
> ➢ "Why you won't even consider this option?"
> ➢ "Why you quit your job without first talking to me?"
> ➢ "Why you use sarcasm?"

In these situations, the tension is already intense and can quickly escalate into a relationship-destroying brawl. You are fighting for air, and these opening words are a strong faith statement that you will not overreact. They also buy you some time to calm down and truly listen.

This works!

The correct opening words are stunning in power. They quickly become a habit because they are so effective. Beth and I have cancelled thousands of arguments by opening our dialogue with these words.

Now the door is open to hear Jesus' heart through them.

After this powerful, godly, opening question, the other person will often share with you their positive passions.

Almost every person has some positive passions, even when their actions are terribly wrong. If we listen carefully to their response, they will give us hints about why they did what they did.

This is our opportunity! If we will now press forward into Jesus, we will clearly hear his heart through this person and learn some life-changing truths.

4

Step Two -
The Listening Test

The bravest words ever spoken

It only takes one minute to immediately calm our own anger. It only takes one minute to begin to understand someone else's perspective. These brave words work every time.

Unfortunately, most people don't have the courage to utter these words. I've seen these words turn the strongest, boldest men into whimpering cowards. I've seen these words turn the most confident adults into insecure children. Many selfish people simply refuse to utter these words.

As soon as I verbalize these words, my ignorance is exposed. Everyone will immediately see whether I have listened well. It will be obvious to the whole world. These words are harder to utter than an apology. These words take massive doses of humility.

Because these words take more humility than any other sentence spoken between humans, most proud people vehemently hate these words. They despise them! They ridicule them! They turn red with rage if you ask them to say these words.

These words are… *"If I hear your heart, your PASSIONS are…"*

In our church we call these words "The Listening Test."

Once we utter these words, we place ourselves in the most vulnerable position possible between two human beings. We agree to expose our blindness to another person. We submit to learn from this person. We have given this person the final authority to evaluate our listening skills.

Everyone assumes he understands the other person's viewpoint. Only a humble person is willing to be tested on whether he has perceived accurately.

The reason a proud person hates these words so vehemently is because he does not want to understand the other person's perspective. He does not care! He does not want truth. He only wants to win the argument.

> *A fool finds no pleasure in understanding*
> *but delights in airing his own opinions. Proverbs 18:2*

Although the listening test takes effort to learn, it is extremely pleasing to Jesus.

> *This is the one I esteem:*
> *he who is humble and contrite in spirit, and trembles at my word. Isaiah 66:2*

Passions vs. actions

Almost everyone has some godly passions in their heart when they take an action. The action may have been irritating, foolish, or evil, but some of the passions behind these actions may be godly.

A father may have a godly passion to build discipline and strength into his son. He may be overly harsh, sarcastic, or cutting with his words. His godly passion was corrupted by wrong methods.

A mother may have a godly passion to be loving, kind, and affirming toward her child. In her actions, she may spoil a selfish child. Her godly passion was corrupted by poor training and resulted in wrong actions.

Our marriage was doomed.

The heart of the listening test is to turn a dialogue from an adversarial, horizontal debate between 2 people to a vertical harmony of 2 people trying to hear Jesus' heart together.

If my wife and I are having a discussion, and she makes a statement that irritates me, I might find that in her statement:

➢ 30% of what she said was based out of a wrong attitude or a false assumption.
➢ 50% of what she said was useless information.
➢ 20% of what she said contained a valuable insight.

In my own power, I would overreact to the first 80%.

However, because I prayed on my belt that day, I am able to bypass the first 80% and look for what Jesus is trying to teach me through the other 20%.

I have another way of verbalizing the listening test. I often say, *"What I hear Jesus saying through you to me is…"*

Bringing Jesus directly into the conversation changes everything.

Beth and I were not raised this way. Beth was raised in a home where communication on serious issues was ignored. They lived by the rule of silence. Beth is a quiet, gentle soul who can tend to avoid issues.

I was raised in a home where communication on serious issues was handled by screaming and cussing at the top of our lungs. My personality is very verbal, highly productive, and aggressive.

Psychologists would have told you that our marriage was doomed from the beginning. The Belt of Truth cancelled that curse by teaching us how to communicate.

Beth's and my passions

My wife, Beth's, primary passions are peace and gentleness.

My primary passions are helping people and analyzing to understand why people react as they do.

When we first married, Beth enjoyed helping people and learning, but she was not nearly as passionate in these areas as I was. If someone did not want help, she was fine to walk away. She did not want to analyze everyone. She simply wanted peace. That was unfathomable to me. I could not even imagine moving on from a situation without understanding. To give up without trying to help and understand felt like giving up oxygen.

In the early years, I enjoyed peace, but I did not feel that it was always worth the effort of gentleness and kindness. I did not mind rocking the boat and stirring relational waters if I could help someone and learn something. This bothered Beth deeply! Her life theme is, "Don't rock the boat!" Many times I charged forward and stirred up dust in a situation because I saw something wrong. I wanted to right the wrongs and help people, whether they asked for help or not. When my actions removed peace from a situation, Beth felt as though I were taking away her oxygen.

Because of the listening test, I spoke aloud, many times, the validity, wisdom, and truth I found in Beth's passions. The more I affirmed Beth's passions for peace and gentleness, the more I saw the validity of peace and gentleness as Biblical attitudes. I eventually learned that Jesus wanted to increase my passion for peace and gentleness.

This made all the difference. I was no longer guarding peace and trying to be gentle just to please Beth. I was hearing Jesus' heart for me and learning how he wanted to change me. I will probably never be as naturally gentle as Beth. However I am now 1,000 times gentler because I found more of Jesus' heart through Beth's passions. Hearing Jesus' heart through Beth's passions allowed me to grow in my walk with Jesus and helped me to become a better counselor.

Because of the listening test, Beth understood that Jesus wanted to increase her passion for helping people and understanding their reactions. Beth will never be as naturally eager to get involved and analyze as I am. However, she grows more like Jesus in these areas every year.

We did not change quickly. It took decades! We guarded each other in our hot spots because we understood the godly passions behind them.

Here is the funny part! We both found more success in our primary passions because of our mate's passions.

I have much more permanent success in helping people now because I give them space and am gentler. Beth now understands that dealing well with issues produces more permanent peace.

Other people's passions teach us more about Jesus' heart and give us more success in life.

We may still be irritated after step 1.

In step 1, we learned to open a tense dialogue with the gracious words: *"Can you please help me to understand why you…?"*

Once the other person has answered our opening question, the fire of frustration may still be burning in our hearts. Sometimes their answer irritates us even more.

After this opening question, we must choose between Jesus and our flesh. If we love Jesus, we bend down and immerse our hand further into the bucket of the water of Jesus' love. We extend our hand deeper into the bucket of water by saying the word, *"If I hear your heart, your passions are...."*

The listening test melts hearts.

The listening test melts the other person's heart! Nothing encourages an individual as much as another human being trying to understand their passions. Our passions are the deep rivers that motivate all of our actions. People will gladly change their actions if they believe that there is a more effective way of fulfilling their passions.

When doing the listening test, the word "passions" is essential. Passion is always understood as a positive word. It is impossible to say the word "passion" out loud without stating some kind, affirming motivation in the other person.

When we correctly guess the other person's positive passions, it greatly softens our own hearts and helps us to hear what Jesus may be trying to teach us through them.

Step 1 and step 2 are intimately connected.

If we listen carefully, after we say, *"Can you please help me to understand why you...?"* we will hear the person express their passions. Their answer will reveal their motivations. They will tell you "why" they did what they did. They will say words such as:

> ➢ *"I was hoping to help..."*
> ➢ *"I wanted to avoid..."*
> ➢ *"I was trying to give..."*

If we listen carefully, we can find the reason why they did this action and discover a positive passion that describes their motivation. When we have identified their passion, we have struck gold. Remember that most people will change their actions if they believe there is a better way to achieve their passions.

When we hear our own mouth describe the godly passions that motivated their actions, the torch is underwater, our ears are open to Jesus, and our hearts are soft toward this person. Their actions make sense to us in the light of their passions.

When the listening test is complete, I like you again!

Don't bother doing the listening test unless you are determined to like the person again by the time you are done talking. If this is not your goal, just walk away and give them space.

The listening test is hard work because it exposes our hearts. Our flesh desires to attack and expose the ugly things in their hearts. The Spirit of God within us wants to teach us something fascinating through them.

> *The purposes of a person's heart are deep waters,*
> *but one who has insight draws them out. Proverbs 20:5*

It feels much easier to simply throw the torch toward the gas. Bending down and immersing our hand in water can be uncomfortable, but it is very rewarding.

Here is how I pray on the Belt of Truth.

When I daily pray on my belt, I begin by asking myself how many times yesterday I used the listening test. My prayer time is my accountability time.

As I begin to pray over the upcoming day, I mentally take this belt, and I loop it under each belt loop. The belt coming under each loop is my picture of humility. I'm coming under the other person's perspective.

The first belt loop is always my wife.

My wife and I have used the listening test most every day for over 35 years. We have amazing, pleasant conversations. We resolve misunderstandings almost immediately.

Both of my children tell me that the reason they walk with Jesus as adults is because of the communication and love they saw between

Beth and me in our marriage. The listening test saved the souls of my children!

My word choices are extremely important when I pray.

> ➤ "Jesus, please help me to hear your heart through my wife today…

> ➤ And to really listen."

The phrase "really listen" is code for, *"Lord, please help me to use the listening test multiple times today with Beth."*

The rest of my belt

After I have prayed to hear more of Jesus' heart through my wife's perspective, I do the same thing for the remaining five belt loops of my:

1. adult children,
2. staff & church family,
3. emails,
4. appointments, and
5. divine appointments God has for me that day.

By the time I have come under these belt loops, I am excited to watch for opportunities to do the listening test that day.

Conclusions

At this point you understand how to have a great opening line, which is step 1. If you are still irritated after step 1, a humble person would move on to step 2.

Although steps 1 and 2 calm the tension, the issue is not resolved until you have added step 3.

Step 3 may surprise you!

5

Step Three -

Be Secure!

When Wimps become Leaders!

Latching the belt

Latching the belt is the 3rd step.

> *Having girded your loins with truth… Ephesians 6:14 (NAS)*

What an interesting phrase, "Gird your loins." What does it mean? "Gird your loins" is an idiom or colloquialism, which is a phrase that takes on a special meaning within the local culture in which it is used. Idioms and colloquialisms are rich, colorful expressions that are pregnant with meaning and emotion.

In the Hebrew and Greek cultures of Biblical times, the colloquialism, "Gird your loins" specifically meant, "Be direct!"

Repeatedly, scripture is clear that you cannot be a person of truth unless you are willing "to be direct."

Understanding the culture

In Biblical times, virtually no one wore pants!

The Iron Age would later bring an abundance of needles and thread so that tailored clothes, such as pants, could be readily available. From the time of Adam through the life of Paul, most people wore outfits that looked like robes. These were full-length garments that hung down to a man's calves or ankles. They were comfortable and easy to make with one piece of material.

This robe-like apparel was cumbersome in hand-to-hand combat. The long, flowing material around your legs could hinder your movement and even cause you to trip or fall. In a fight, lack of mobility with your legs could be fatal.

When preparing to engage in battle, it was a common practice to gather up the extraneous cloth from around your legs and wrap it around your waist.

In essence, you would turn the bottom half of your robe into a pair of shorts.

This practice of tightly wrapping the excess material around your waist to prepare for battle was called "Girding your loins."

It was from this usage that "Gird your loins!" developed into an imperative command to "Be direct!" The concept being that verbal warfare is similar to physical warfare. In verbal warfare, you gather up all long, flowing, extraneous thoughts, and you tie them down. You tie down all hesitancy, rabbit trails, and minor subjects, and you beeline to the main issue. You get direct!

There are 3 different scripture passages that emphasize this idiom.

The book of Job is dominated by an argument. From chapters 2 - 37, the book is filled with Job debating with 4 of his friends.

Their basic complaint against Job is, "You must have sin in your life. That's the only reason all of these bad things could be happening to you." They want Job to repent and ask God's forgiveness for all of his terrible sins so that these bad things will stop happening to him.

Job, on the other hand, is quite certain that he has done nothing wrong. As the tension escalates, he gets progressively more vehement that God is treating him unfairly. Ultimately, his stance becomes, "If I could talk to God directly, he would have to answer some tough questions from me."

In Job 38, God shows up and gives Job the chance to ask his tough questions.

> *Then the Lord answered Job out of the whirlwind and said*
> *"Who is this that darkens counsel by words without knowledge?*
> *Now gird up your loins like a man,*
> *and I will ask you, and you instruct Me." Job 38:1-3 (NAS)*

In this context, it's very obvious that God is meeting Job's challenge. He says to Job, "Here I am! You wanted to get direct with me! Here's your chance. I'll ask you the questions, and you teach me!"

For 2 chapters, God asks questions. At the end of these questions in chapter 40, God challenges Job to be direct with him.

> *Then the Lord said to Job,*
> *"Will the faultfinder contend with the Almighty?*
> *Let him who reproves God answer it." Job 40:1-2 (NAS)*

Job responds that he should have kept his mouth shut.

> *Then Job answered the Lord and said, "Behold, I am insignificant; what can I*
> *reply to You? Once I have spoken, and I will not answer;*
> *even twice, and I will add nothing more." Job 40:3-5 (NAS)*

Amazingly, Job dropping the argument is not good enough for God. He is not willing for Job to just stop talking. God wants the issue resolved.

He again tells Job to "Gird his loins," and be direct with God.

> *Then the Lord answered Job out of the storm and said,*
> *"Now gird up your loins like a man;*
> *I will ask you and you instruct Me." Job 40:6-7 (NAS)*

A third example of "Gird your loins" is found in Jeremiah. God commissions Jeremiah to be a prophet to the nation of Judah. Jeremiah is afraid to speak to Judah's leaders. God tells Jeremiah to get direct and say whatever he tells him to say.

> *Now, gird up your loins and arise, and*
> *speak to them all which I command you. Jeremiah 1:17 (NAS)*

Now, let's look at why Paul chose this colorful phrase about plain talk to teach us how to be people of truth.

An unlatched belt is not secure.

If someone walked into a meeting completely dressed except that he had not latched his belt, people in the room would feel awkward. The individual may be modestly dressed. He may even be clothed in an expensive outfit. However, it is embarrassing to everyone that he has woven a belt through all belt loops and has not buckled the belt.

In the same way, when someone uses the listening test to make others happy but does not bring resolution for everyone, it makes others feel awkward. The process of buckling the Belt of Truth has not been completed.

People-pleasers do not find truth.

"People-pleaser" is a counseling term for a person who strains to make everyone else happy in conflicts. They hate all arguments. They want the tension to just go away. They don't "resolve" issues.

They just try harder to make everyone happy. Every time a people-pleaser gives in to others in order to avoid strife, he pats himself on the back and congratulates himself that he is so godly! People-pleasers love the listening test. They are eager to make others happy. Sadly, I've seen 2 things that can happen to the people-pleaser who believes that trying hard to please everyone is godly.

1. He cracks up.

> He has tried hard to placate everyone one thousand times, one million times, 10 million times. He has this vain hope that if he just keeps trying to make everyone happy, they will return the favor. He becomes more controlled, confused, deceived, and helpless. He may wind up on anti-depressant drugs.

2. He blows up.

> Each time he tries harder to please, he resents it more. After this unfair treatment has built up, in his mind, to a cruel level, he blows up! He explodes and releases outbursts of anger. He no longer wants honest discussion. He just wants everybody to give into him! He's been giving in for so long that he feels that it's his turn. After a time of being an ugly, angry person, his drowning guilt swings him back to the opposite extreme of his people-pleasing reactions.

The startling application of Ephesians 6:14 is that, in conflicts with other people, just hearing other's hearts or pleasing others is not godly. You cannot be both a people-pleaser and a person of truth!

➢ Humility, truly understanding the other person's perspective, is the beginning of resolving a conflict.

➢ However, to have truth, you have to be secure enough to calmly and graciously be direct.

Latch the belt – be a leader!

Fastening a belt is not complete until the belt pulls back far enough to cause mild tension in the opposite direction and then locks into a position that is comfortable for all points along the belt. The opposing tension reminds us that hearing other people's hearts is not our goal. Our goal is to hear Jesus' heart together.

Thus, after I have heard someone's heart, I must now ask Jesus what insight I can add that can help us both hear Jesus' heart together.

"Wishing" vs. "Training"

In my own life, the concept of "training" attitudes into my immediate environment completely redirected all of my nearest relationships.

Having spent the first 40 years of my life "wishing" others would reciprocate my eagerness to hear their hearts, by listening to me, I was a frenetic, fragile, disappointed soul.

I have spent the last 20 years "training" those closest to me to listen, after I have heard their hearts. I have learned to be a leader. A wise leader seeks to create a refuge of active listeners who are the ultimate safe teammates. This is his condition for close friends.

Every office, family, and friendship has distinctive cultural traits. We may be limited in our ability to change the culture of our nation, but we have great power to adjust the inherent attitudes within our immediately family, friendships and work environment.

This change of focus from wishing to be heard, toward buckling my belt and training those closest to me to be excellent listeners has steadily restored my soul. I now have much more calmness, steadiness, patience, confidence and hope.

When I first began to train others, requiring them to listen was a completely new concept to me. "Girding my loins" required me to pretend that I was a confident person. I began to look for points of confidence.

Confidence point # 1 - You are blessed to have me as a friend!

Active listeners are a rare species. People are drawn to us. We do not lack for those who want to be our friends. By using the listening test daily in non-tension situations, active listeners build a debt of love with most acquaintances. When we have heard their hearts regularly, they know that we sincerely care about them.

This high level of graciousness gives us confidence. True listening and caring are extremely scarce traits in our self-centered world.

Over 40 years, I slowly began to see that it was not arrogance for me to recognize that others were blessed to have my friendship. I deeply love my friends. I constantly seek to affirm, serve, and encourage them. In misunderstandings, I am eager to hear their heart and hear Jesus through them.

This growth of a backbone helped me to understand that I did not have to explode when others were abusing me. I simply needed to withdraw the privilege of my friendship. I learned to withdraw friendship incrementally and gradually.

This epiphany led to my second growth point of confidence.

Confidence point # 2 - Calm, lighthearted, and charming

Being direct does not require being abrasive!

After 4 decades wishing others would reciprocate my kindness, warmth, and desire to listen, I found myself emotionally unstable, anxious, confused, and embittered.

When I changed my focus toward becoming a leader, I learned to win a person's heart and then turn on the charm. Once I have won their heart, I smile and ask them if I may share an insight that could help us both. I discovered that I could be secure and direct without being rude or angry.

The Belt of Truth is not a game of "Your Turn/My Turn." After I hear someone's heart, I do not gleefully erupt with my built-up tensions.

My goal is not to get a chance to be honest. My goal is for us to hear Jesus' heart together. I look for the one point in my perspective that they can grasp, which will most help us come into agreement and move closer to Jesus' heart.

Confidence point # 3 - It all begins with prayer.

This is all theory to me until I pray. Having spent 40 years as a people-pleaser, it is still the first reaction of my soul. However, God's armor strengthens me to choose his reactions over my fleshly responses.

After bringing my belt under each belt loop in prayer, I end by mentally connecting the ends of the belt together. In that action, I ask the Lord to give me a gracious heart to be secure today. I ask the Lord to help me be alert to the times when I am listening with a heart to please, rather than a heart to draw us both closer to Jesus.

I also ask the Lord to remind me that unresolved issues always return. I want to permanently remove the distraction of tension and move forward with God's purposes in my life.

Confidence point # 4 - Not everyone is trainable.

The next weapon of God's armor, the Breastplate of Righteousness, teaches us when to put more space between critical-controlling people and ourselves. The Breastplate of Righteousness helps to set us free from trying too hard to please others.

The Belt of Truth has to come first. The Belt of Truth gives us a clear conscience that we have done a good job of trying to communicate. That makes it much easier to walk away when necessary.

Confidence point # 5 - Guide through the listening test

No one becomes a great leader until they are great at listening. The listening test involves being able to read and understand people. Leaders remove confusion, build team, understand people, and are able to find solutions that bring permanent peace to everyone on the team. Leaders comfortably wear the mantle of productivity. Leaders see strife as a major distraction and an immense waste of time.

When I became skilled at the listening test, I realized that I usually had 3 to 4 different ways I could successfully repeat back a person's heart. Any of those responses would thrill the other person.

As a leader, I began to experiment with phrasing the listening test in ways that moved us both closer to resolution. I melted their heart while also moving them closer to my perspective. I was able to affirm their passion and then doubly affirm that I had the same passion. I then shared other passions I had which might help them to understand my heart. Sharing passions calmed the dialogue and increased understanding. We could then discuss alternative actions that might satisfy both of our passions.

When I realized that the listening test could guide a person toward truth and bring very quick, deep unity, it became my most cherished weapon. It made me eager to use the listening test in every key conversation.

20 years later, I am undistracted by strife.

As I approach 60 years old, my only goal is to bear fruit for my king. Having a strife-free life is heavenly. It permits me to focus all of my emotional energy on God's kingdom.

Charmaine

Charmaine was stuck! Her life was perfect in so many ways. She loved Jesus passionately. She loved her church. She was faithful to pray on God's armor every morning while getting ready for work. She really loved working at the adoption agency. She had been there 2 years and had gotten great reviews. She loved helping people.

If only she didn't have 2 issues in her life! She yearned for Jesus to send her a husband, and she had asked Jesus many times to please help Antoine retire so she wouldn't have to work with him.

When she was first hired, Antoine had already worked there for many years. He was 30 years older than she was and more experienced, so she didn't mind when he told her where she needed to improve. Charmaine constantly prayed that Jesus would keep her humble. Some of Antoine's suggestions were good. Because she prayed on God's armor, Charmaine would often repeat back Antoine's heart to make sure she had heard him well. Antoine loved it when Charmaine did the listening test.

Over time though, as she got better at her job, she hoped that he would stop giving her the benefit of his wisdom. Unfortunately, Antoine still came by regularly to evaluate her. He was not her superior. In fact, Charmaine guessed that their boss also hoped that Antoine would retire this year.

Yesterday, Antoine told her that he had decided to stay on one more year. Charmaine was depressed and angry as she began her prayer time. "Lord, I work really hard to be gracious and kind to everyone. I want to let you shine through me. Is it too much to ask for you to remove this one person? I have been extremely patient. Please, Lord, can't you help me with this one thing?"

The more she prayed this way, the worse she felt, so Charmaine began to praise the Lord and draw near by the blood of Jesus. As she began to put on the armor, she got stuck on the Belt of Truth. Charmaine felt the Lord nudging her to latch her belt. Charmaine faced the truth she had avoided for 2 years. She cried out, "Lord, do you really want me to be direct with Antoine? Oh, sweet Jesus, please help me."

Charmaine was folding her clothes while praying, but she suddenly dropped to her knees as she continued in prayer. "Precious Jesus, you know I love you. You know how hard this is for me. Please help me, Jesus!" As Charmaine faced the reality of Jesus' direction in her life, she was surprised at the peace she felt.

That day Antoine dropped by her desk to give her more advice. He usually talked for 10 minutes. After a few sentences, Charmaine interrupted Antoine by saying: "Antoine, can you please help me to understand why you give me so much advice?" Antoine quickly responded that he liked to help Charmaine and wanted to see her succeed. Charmaine replied, "If I hear your heart, Antoine, you have a great passion to see me succeed. You are suggesting this change in my phone follow-ups so I can get more done in a shorter amount of time. Have I heard your heart?" Antoine grinned through his verbal agreement.

Charmaine said, "I am a much better worker today because of all of your advice." Taking a deep breath she added, "May I share a thought that may help me to do a better job of receiving your input?" Liking that idea, Antoine eagerly agreed.

She opened with a confession. "This is really hard for me and I am nervous. Please give me a minute to try to express my thoughts." Antoine leaned in with compassion.

Charmaine continued, "I find myself shutting down when I see you coming. I realize that you really care about me and that is why you give me so much advice. However, I give a lot of affirmation to others because I love the idea of affirmation. Also, I would like to believe that I have learned a good bit since I have come here. My passion is affirmation. I thirst to receive affirmation."

Antoine began to back up with an intense look on his face.

Charmaine prayed in her heart, asking for the courage to continue with graciousness. "Antoine I would like to ask 2 favors of you. First, would you always please give me one or 2 positives before you give me any advice? Second, would you please ask me if I would like to hear some advice on a specific area before diving in?"

Charmaine hoped to say more but Antoine interrupted in anger. "That is the thanks I get for trying to help." Antoine blustered as he stormed away.

Charmaine's stomach went to her feet. She thought she might throw up. For the next week or 2, she barely made it through the fog of Antoine's loud displeasure with her. Slowly, though, her soul began to awaken.

Over the next few months, the pain of Antoine's on-going rejection began to fade. The surprise benefit was that Charmaine found herself making more friends at her job. It seemed that there were healthy souls simply waiting for her to join them.

Eventually, Antoine and Charmaine established a somewhat formal, cordial working relationship. By the time he retired, a measure of warmth had been restored to their talks. Charmaine found it easy to praise Antoine on his accomplishments once she no longer desired his approval.

Even more profound, Charmaine began to understand that she had not been ready to get married earlier. She had not been a healthy soul. Charmaine began to see God's plan for her life. She was no longer stuck.

Prayers answered immediately

Charmaine discovered that Jesus could answer a prayer immediately and slowly at the same time. Jesus was willing to wait until she was ready to hear his truth.

6

Step Four -

Short Term Solutions

We heard each other's hearts, but we still disagree!

We are both humble and secure. We really listened to each other, but we still differ on the solution. What do we do next? I have heard that question hundreds of times. Thankfully, finding solutions is easy if you mix in a little wisdom with the Belt of Truth.

The secret is to avoid looking for permanent solutions and seek instead to take one small step forward. Call it research. With a short-term experiment we can quickly gain success and momentum toward agreement.

The entire theme of this book is that God answers our prayers immediately by showing us the next step.

This small point of insight opens the door to the idea of short-term experiments that act as research toward long-term solutions. These short-term experiments bring progress and give us confidence that we are hearing God clearly.

The psalmist talks about God's revelation as a "One step at a time" process.

> *Your word is a lamp for my feet, a light on my path. Psalm 119:105*

In the book of Daniel, we find the idea of a short-term experiment as a temporary solution. Daniel did not want to eat the food of the Babylonians. He needed a solution that made everyone happy. His brilliant suggestion of a 10 day test solved the conflict.

> *But Daniel resolved not to defile himself with the royal food and wine, and he asked the chief official for permission not to defile himself this way. [9] Now God had caused the official to show favor and compassion to Daniel, [10] but the official told Daniel, "I am afraid of my lord the king, who has assigned your food and drink. Why should he see you looking worse than the other young men your age? The king would then have my head because of you."*
>
> *[11] Daniel then said to the guard whom the chief official had appointed over Daniel, Hananiah, Mishael and Azariah,*
>
> *[12] "Please test your servants for ten days:*
>
> *Give us nothing but vegetables to eat and water to drink. [13] Then compare our appearance with that of the young men who eat the royal food, and treat your servants in accordance with what you see."*
>
> *[14] So he agreed to this and tested them for ten days.*
>
> *[15] At the end of the ten days they looked healthier and better nourished than any of the young men who ate the royal food. [16] So the guard took away their choice food and the wine they were to drink and gave them vegetables instead.*
> *Daniel 1:8-16*

Daniel was so wise. He did not push for an immediate, permanent answer. He did not increase the tension.

By suggesting a short-term experiment, he made an ally of his boss and let the Lord show himself strong in Daniel's life.

In many conflicts, there is no instant, long-lasting solution. There is no single brilliant idea that will solve everything. God wants us to learn from trying short-term experiments and gleaning wisdom from each point of progress.

Once we shift the focus away from trying to find a permanent solution, everyone relaxes. It is easy to find a temporary idea that gives everyone a positive step forward.

Examples of short-term experiments

We have heard each other's hearts, but we still disagree over:

1. <u>Should we buy a new car or keep our old car?</u>
   - ➢ Let's try to save an extra $400 a month for 3 months.
   - ➢ That experiment will let us know if we can afford a new car payment.

2. <u>What should we do about the constant extended family strife?</u>
   - ➢ Let's limit our time at your parents to 2 hours per visit.
   - ➢ Let's try this for 3 months.
   - ➢ It seems like the arguments and harsh comments start after we have been there for a few hours.

3. <u>Which church should we attend?</u>
   - ➢ Let's go to the church you prefer every week, for 4 weeks.
   - ➢ Then let's go to the church I prefer every week, for 4 weeks.

4. <u>What is the right way to fold the laundry?</u>
   - ➢ Let's experiment with you doing all the laundry for 2 weeks and folding it anyway you like.
   - ➢ After that, I will do all the laundry for 2 weeks and fold it anyway I like.

The instant we begin to look at short-term experiments as a way of solving disagreements, creativity is released. Adversaries become allies. New information is gathered. When I coach senior pastors, I tell them the greatest leadership word they will ever use in their church is the word, "Experiment."

The right way to seek counsel

Once we begin to seek short-term solutions for disagreements, we then become open to receiving input from other people. We feel safe in seeking counsel.

When we ask someone for ideas, we retain the authority to make the final decision. As we feel safe, we can become bold in asking many people for ideas.

Many advisers make victory sure. Proverbs 11:14

Summarizing the Belt of Truth

"In disagreements, I don't have the whole picture!"

That one line sums up our how the Belt of Truth changes our thinking.

The process of resolving misunderstandings is so simple and successful that it becomes intuitive. Because we understand that all conflict is Jesus wanting to teach us something through the other person, we eagerly:

1. Use a great opening question,
2. Find their passions through the listening test,
3. Share our passions and points that bring us together, and
4. Find short-term solutions that guarantee some progress.

The Belt of Truth sets up the Breastplate of Righteousness

The Belt of Truth removes strife from our lives. As we move into the second piece of God's armor, we will see a divine connection between the first 2 pieces of armor.

In a strife-free life, it is much easier to ask God to fill our emotions with his pleasure as we put on the Breastplate of Righteousness.

Emotions

=

Breastplate of Righteousness

7

Feeling
that God Is
Pleased with Me

I was not raised in a home where I felt comfortable in my dad's approval. My dad had extreme rage. For the first 20 years of my life, I never relaxed in his presence for even 10 seconds. I was terrified all the time. I remember being beaten with a board because I shut the door too loudly. I remember being stripped naked and beaten with a large belt because I walked too loudly across the floor or because I didn't move quickly enough when called. I remember being backhanded, almost knocked out, and having no idea what I did wrong. I was just told that I had better shape up. I remember shaking in my dad's presence almost all the time.

With this picture of an earthly father, I found it almost impossible to believe that my heavenly Father was pleased with me.

For 10 years, I choked, sobbed, or hyperventilated when I prayed on the Breastplate of Righteousness. Yet, I knew these prayers were Biblical, so I continued to speak these words. Each time I sobbed out the prayers for this second piece of armor, I knew that God was answering my prayer. I could feel the knots in my heart slowly unwinding. Finally, after 10 years, it was easy to pray on the Breastplate of Righteousness. I was changed from the inside out.

The breastplate is the piece that God designed to guard our hearts. It is the most emotional piece of armor.

"In place" = secure when we fail

...with the breastplate of righteousness in place Ephesians 6:14

The breastplate shelters our emotions when we fail. A secure person is a healthy soul. In telling us about the breastplate, Paul uses the emphatic words, "in place!" He teaches us how to be confident in God's gift of righteousness through the positioning of the breastplate.

In Paul's analogy, each piece of armor has significance.
- ➢ For the Roman soldier, what was the value of his breastplate?
- ➢ In hand-to-hand combat, what was the purpose of his breastplate?
- ➢ In a life or death struggle with the enemy, what was the usefulness of his breastplate?

The best way to grasp the importance of the breastplate is to look at these questions from a different perspective. For the Roman soldier, in a life or death struggle of hand-to-hand combat with the enemy, if he does everything right … does he need his breastplate?

Don't rush through this question. Take your time and think about it. Certainly, every soldier needs his sword to thrust, point, attack, and defend himself in battle. Certainly he needs his shield to protect himself and to batter the enemy. His belt holds his outfit together. His shoes enable him to move quickly and comfortably over rough terrain. His helmet is both an offensive and defensive weapon. But… if he uses each piece of armor perfectly, if he does everything right, does he need his breastplate?

No! If a soldier fights a textbook case of hand-to-hand combat, then he will return to camp without a single scratch on his breastplate.

I only need a breastplate when I do something wrong!

When my Sword of the Spirit misses the mark; when my Shield of Faith drops; when my Helmet of Salvation is turned around and I can't see; when my Shoes of Peace and Readiness don't fit; when my Belt of Truth no longer wraps all the way around me and I trip and fall; when I do something wrong; when I fail; when I am down; when I am vulnerable; when my enemy aims a death thrust at my heart; when I deserve to die….that is when I need my breastplate to protect my heart!

The first thing we learn from the "in place" position of the breastplate is that God's righteousness protects our hearts when we do wrong things.

How do we respond after we repent?

How deeply does shame continue to pierce our hearts after we have repented of doing something wrong?

I am not talking about a healthy sense of conviction that leads us to repentance. I am talking about after we repent.

How long does condemnation stay with us? How often do we beat ourselves up? How does it change our image of ourselves?

The best time to recognize the basis of our identity is after repenting of sin. We've messed up, and we regret it. We've done something stupid, and we are so sorry. These are the times that test whether or not we understand God's righteousness.

Do we understand that God's righteousness is a gift?

A Roman solider had a helper. He had an armor bearer who would guide him in the putting on of each piece of armor. We have a helper too. John 14:26 (NAS) tells us,

> *But the Helper, the Holy Spirit, whom the Father will send in My name, He will teach you all things, and bring to your remembrance all that I said to you.*

The Holy Spirit is our armor bearer who helps us. In Paul's day, each piece of armor was put on through a joint effort between the soldier and his helper. The helper would hand the piece of armor to the soldier. Together, they would strap it in place and make sure it was adjusted properly.

Only one piece of armor was not a mutual effort. With this piece of armor, the soldier's hands were useless, and he was required to stand still and do nothing.

While the armor bearer strapped the breastplate to the chest, the soldier had to stand quietly and receive. This is one of my favorite insights on the Breastplate of Righteousness.

Praise God that we can do nothing to earn God's righteousness!

The books of Romans and Galatians are fantastic explanations of how God's righteousness is a gift to us, paid for by Jesus Christ. God's righteousness is the perfect answer to every wrong thing we have ever done, after we have repented.

After repenting, God's righteousness declares that we are right in His eyes. It doesn't matter to God whether it's a little wrong, a big wrong, or a whole lifetime of wrongs. Once we have confessed and repented of our wrongs, we are able to receive the gift of righteousness, which is received by faith.

Once we receive this gift of righteousness, God looks at our record and declares us spotless and right in his eyes in every way.

God's righteousness declares that you are his son!

You can't earn son-ship. It's a gift.

Being an approved son of God is also the healthiest foundation of identity that any person can possess.

The word "righteousness" is found in the book of Romans 63 times. That is an astounding number of times for a 16 chapter book. Romans and Galatians describe the benefits of receiving the gift of God's righteousness.

> *...you received the Spirit of son-ship. And by Him we cry, "Abba, Father."*
> *Romans 8:15*

> *...lead us to Christ that we might be justified (made righteous) by faith. You are all sons of God through faith in Christ Jesus. Galatians 3:24, 26*

> *...to redeem those under the law, that we might receive the full rights of sons. Because you are sons, God sent the Spirit of his Son into our hearts, the Spirit who calls out, "Abba, Father." So you are no longer a slave, but a son, and since you are a son, God has made you also an heir. Galatians 4:5-7*

Having received God's righteousness, we walk into a room as Princes or Princesses. We are not just any princes or princesses. We are sons and daughters of the King of Kings. We are sons and daughters of the living, eternal, all-powerful God.

God's righteousness declares that God himself thinks you are wonderful!

Romans, the book about God's righteousness, concludes with these famous words:

> *Accept one another, then, just as Christ has accepted you. Romans 15:7*

Look at those last 4 words: *"Christ has accepted you!"*

The Greek word translated "accept" is a forceful, graphic, and descriptive word. It is the word "proslambano."

Proslambano is an emotional word. Proslambano means:

> "To charge straight toward a person
> and to forcefully take him to yourself,
> above or over-riding every other issue."

Proslambano is a picture of God chasing you down to give you a bear hug! This is the picture Jesus presented of our heavenly Father in the parable of the prodigal son.

When we receive God's free gift of righteousness, he is so pleased with us, and he thinks we are so wonderful that he wholeheartedly, cheerfully, and possessively takes us to himself. He proslambanos us!

The phrase "In Place" refers to our emotions.

…with the breastplate of righteousness in place Ephesians 6:14

The phrase "in place" comes from the Greek word "enduo," which means: "to fill within, fitting perfectly and in a state of complete rest." Enduo is a fluid, gentle, flowing word relating to emotions.

The Breastplate of Righteousness is a plate over our breast. That is what a "breastplate" is. It's so strong and impenetrable that no arrow of Satan can pierce it. This was too cold and impersonal for the Apostle Paul. To complete the picture, he added the very soft, inward, personal word "enduo."

What a brilliant man the Apostle Paul was! To explain to us how God's righteousness affects our lives, he added another word that talks about our emotions.

God's righteousness is a powerful, unbreakable, impenetrable plate over our hearts. Yet, God's righteousness is also (enduo) a river that rises within us, fitting perfectly and bringing our emotions into a state of complete rest. Do you catch the significance of this?

➢ We are right in His eyes.

He wants us to feel *(enduo - rising deep within our hearts, where it fits perfectly, and we come to a state of complete rest)* that we are right in his eyes.

➢ We are his sons and daughters.

He wants us to feel *(enduo - rising deep within our hearts, where it fits perfectly, and we come to a state of complete rest)* that we are his sons and daughters.

➢ He thinks we are wonderful.

He wants us to feel *(enduo - rising deep within our hearts, where it fits perfectly, and we come to a state of complete rest)* that he thinks we are wonderful!

Drink as long as you are thirsty.

In John 7:37-39, Jesus said that we are to drink of the Holy Spirit. In Romans 8:15, the Holy Spirit is called the "Spirit of Sonship." In Psalm 23:5, David said that he was aware of whether his soul was empty or full. He said that he drank of God's Spirit until the inward cup of his soul overflowed.

When I put on the Breastplate of Righteousness, I drink of the Spirit of Sonship until my emotions are filled with God's pleasure. Praying on the breastplate aloud is a huge part of inner healing for many people. I urge you to drink until your cup is overflowing.

Here are some of the prayers I speak out.

➢ I am lost to self and found in you. I live for you and you live through me. I receive the free gift of your righteousness on me, in me, and through me because of the finished work of Jesus. I drink of the Spirit of Sonship by Romans 8:15.

➤ I drink of your acceptance (proslambano) on me, in me, and through me by Romans 15:7.

➤ I drink of your approval on me, in me, and through me by II Timothy 2:15.

➤ I drink of your delight on me, in me, and through me by Psalm 16:3 and Proverbs 3:12.

➤ I drink of your pleasure on me, in me, and through me by Ephesians 1:5.

➤ I drink of your quiet, peaceful confidence on me, in me, and through me by Isaiah 32:17.

My Parched Soul

I recently was unable to have my normal prayer time for 2 full days. This had not happened to me in many years.

By the second day, I was foggy, irritable, unproductive and empty. I had forgotten how miserable it is to try to live the Christian life in my own power. I felt like a total failure to everyone, but especially to God.

On the third morning, I felt like a man who had been in the desert for weeks with no water. On that third day, I spent hours saying each truth out loud and drinking in each one. I said them again and again. I quoted these scriptures until they quenched my thirst. I exhaled long sighs. I felt the tension leave my body. I felt the temptation of trying to work hard to earn God's approval leave my soul.

After 25 years, I need God's armor everyday more than ever.

Rick

Rick finally understood. For many years, he had faithfully prayed on God's armor.

Rick never knew his dad. The man simply did not care. Rick's mom worked 2 jobs to provide for Rick and his sister. She was never home.

When Rick thought of God as his father, he did not have bad memories. He simply had a hole in his heart. He felt like someone had asked him to draw a picture of a Martian. He had no idea what to draw.

In the early years of praying on the breastplate, Rick slowly began to feel the hole close. He began to feel the pleasure of his heavenly Father. Faithfully each day, he spoke out loud the words of receiving his heavenly Father's approval, pleasure, and delight. It was like a water hose filling a large swimming pool. Gently the water began to rise.

Today though, Rick understood. In some ways, he felt like he had never fully fathomed God's pleasure over him until now.

Today, as Rick stood in that hospital room and the doctor handed him his newborn son, he got it. He saw now that his heavenly Father's pleasure and delight in him is not a full swimming pool. It is an ocean. It is a universe of oceans.

Today, he felt his heavenly Father's delight flowing through him. He knew what it felt like to be a dad.

Jesus' words

In the story of the prodigal son, Jesus showed us how eager our heavenly Father is to pour out his pleasure.

> *So he got up and went to his father.*
> *"But while he was still a long way off,*
> *his father saw him and*
> *was filled with compassion for him;*
> *he ran to his son,*
> *threw his arms around him*
> *and kissed him. Luke 15:20*

We can never imagine how greatly our heavenly Father's heart burns to fill our hearts with his pleasure. Jesus died so that our heavenly Father could draw us to himself in a massive hug.

8

How to
Conquer Sin

How can I feel God's pleasure when I have so much filthy sin in my life?

I sincerely want to stop: being angry, doing drugs, being lazy, lusting, cussing, being negative, being selfish, etc. I try so hard to change. The harder I try, the more I seem to fail.

Why do we sin?

That's an easy question to answer. We sin because we believe the sin will be rewarding or satisfying. We think that lusting is rewarding. We suppose that cussing will satisfy us. We hope that being lazy will make us happier. Every person from Eve until today, in every single instance of sin, believed the sin would be more rewarding and satisfying than the ways of God.

Think about some of your strongest sin habits. At the instant you were about to sin, didn't the sin seem to be the easiest and most rewarding path? At that instant, didn't the ways of God seem hard and painful? The root of all sin is a lie that says, "This sin will satisfy me."

Sin…deceived me, and…put me to death. Romans 7:11

But in order that sin might be recognized as sin it produced death in me. Romans 7:13

This is why conquering sin starts with asking God to open our eyes.

The central theme of Roman 6 - 8 is that
  ➢ Everything of sin produces death in me, and
  ➢ Everything of God produces life in me!

When I put on the breastplate, I ask God to open my eyes so I may clearly see how each selfish sin will produce death in me. I also ask God to show me today how his ways will produce life.

I name specific sin patterns in my life. I focus on the areas of selfishness that I tend to repeat. As I ask God to open my eyes in these areas, I can feel myself changing on the inside.

Death

Sin usually starts out as fun and easy, but the longer it lasts, the more miserable we become. Our lives become harder and emptier.

Sin producing "death" is found 31 times in Romans 6 and 7.

Paul points out that the whole reason we became Christians was because we saw 2 things clearly:

1. We looked at ourselves and saw how much our sinful selfishness produced misery, pain, and an empty and shallow existence (death).

2. Then we saw how Jesus' joyful, sweet, and effective life could fill us.

We died to the power of sin to control us and came alive through the life of Jesus.

Let's look at some of the verses that talk about our eyes being opened to see that sin produces a downward spiral to death in us.

...Sin which leads to death Romans 6:16

...You used to offer the parts of your body in slavery to impurity and to ever-increasing wickedness. Romans 6:19

What benefit did you reap at that time from the things you are now ashamed of? Those things result in death. Romans 6:21

For the wages of sin is death. Romans 6:23

...We bore fruit for death. Romans 7:5

...Sin sprang to life and I died. Romans 7:9

Sin deceived me. Romans 7:11

But in order that sin might be recognized as sin, it produced death in me. Romans 7:13

We can see this death in other people's lives.

➢ Drug addicts
   Our hearts break with the pain of their self-destruction.
➢ Sexually immoral souls
   We weep over their emptiness and inability to have real relationships.
➢ Angry people who spend their lives blaming others
   Our hearts ache at how their rage drives everyone away.
➢ Self-pitying, complaining individuals
   We grieve over their deceived, joyless, thankless lives.

When we ask God to open our eyes to see the death in our personal sin habits and selfish patterns:

- ➢ We are horrified!
- ➢ We feel as if we are being swallowed by hell itself.
- ➢ We see the desolation, blaming, misery, and pain that have already come into our lives from our selfishness.
- ➢ We see future anguish that selfishness could bring.
- ➢ There is no longer anything attractive in this sin, and we want to run away.

Life

God's path can sometimes be hard and painful in the first few steps, but, even then, we can clearly see that it will eventually become increasingly joyful, steadily easier, and consistently more productive.

The life God gives is sweet, fulfilling, strong, and calm.

In Romans 6:1 to 8:13, we see the word "life" a total of 31 times.

In the original Greek language, the article "the" is not in John 14:6. Thus, Jesus literally said, "I am life!" Jesus is not one way to have life. He is the only source of life. What do we think of when we hear the word "life"? What do these expressions mean to us?

- ➢ He's the life of the party.
- ➢ You are so full of life.
- ➢ I feel so alive!

These phrases fill us with pictures of vibrancy, energy, fulfillment and joy. Jesus is the only source of life. When we see all self-rule as death, then we can see that Jesus is the only source of vibrancy, energy, fulfillment, and joy.

Let's read a few beautiful scriptures about how Jesus gives us life.

...We too may live a new life. Romans 6:4

...The gift of God is eternal life. Romans 6:23

...The Spirit of life set me free. Romans 8:2

...The mind controlled by the Spirit is life and peace. Romans 8:6

...Your spirit is alive because of righteousness. Romans 8:10

...will also give life to your mortal bodies Romans 8:11

...You will live. Romans 8:13

Don't these verses taste delicious? Let's sample a few others.

The thief comes only in order that he may steal and may kill and may destroy. I have come that they may have and enjoy life, and have it in abundance to the full, till it overflows. John 10:10 (AMP)

...That they may take hold of the life that is truly life. 1 Timothy 6:19

It is not enough to see the emptiness and misery of sin.

Jesus also wants us to see the rich, rewarding lives he has for us. He wants to show us the sweetness of humility, the power of love, the rewards of faithfulness, and the joy of encouraging others.

Jesus wants us to be excited about his plans for our lives.

If we ask Jesus to open our eyes to see life and death, we are halfway to the point of breaking our sin habits.

Pour your nature through me so I want to do right.

After I ask Jesus to open my eyes to see life and death, I ask the Spirit of Sonship to pour the nature of Jesus through me, so I will have the strength and desire to walk in life.

II Peter 1 makes a profound statement. Peter tells us that Jesus' righteousness causes God's very nature to flow through us. This nature changes the desires and yearnings within us. We no longer crave selfishness. We are excited to walk in God's way of life.

*To those who through the righteousness of our God and Savior Jesus Christ
have received a faith as precious as ours… you may **participate** in the
divine nature and escape the corruption in the world caused by evil desires.
II Peter 1:1, 4*

The Holy Spirit living through us is God himself changing our
desires. When I invite the Spirit on Sonship to pour the very nature
of God through my soul, it is more than just seeing life and death. I
now earnestly and passionately desire his plan. I want it more than
anything. I receive his joy, strength, and desire to walk in the
direction of life.

This explains the transition from Romans 7 to 8.

In Romans 7:15-25, Paul describes a man who sees that sin
produces death in him and that God's ways will produce life … but
the man lacks the power to do the right thing.

It is the ultimate frustration to see life and death and be unable to
choose life. This classic passage has awakened millions of Christians
to their need to be able to do more than just see life and death. We
need the very nature of God, by the Holy Spirit, flowing through us
to give us strength to be able to walk in life.

In chapter 8, Paul is going to answer the question of how to have
the power to do right. His answer is the Holy Spirit.

After only mentioning the Spirit a total of 4 times in the 7 full
chapters of Romans 1-7, Paul refers to the Holy Spirit 22 times in
the single chapter of Romans 8.

The Holy Spirit is God's very nature living through us, giving us
God's strength and desire to walk in life.

I feel so much power when I pray these prayers.

1. "Spirit of Sonship, please fill me with your passion, joy, and
    strength to charge forward in the direction of your life."

2. "I claim the very nature of Jesus flowing through me to have the power to walk in God's life!"

I am changed immediately!

When I don't get filled with Jesus' righteousness, I find myself struggling with selfishness all day long. What is worse, I often discover that I have been selfish without even realizing it. My eyes have been closed.

When I do get filled with Jesus' righteousness, I have an easy day. I want to bless others. I enjoy being kind, gracious, and giving. Every aspect of selfishness seems repulsive, and walking in life is easy.

I love daily experiencing God's power to change me through prayer.

Annette

Annette had too many sins to count. She was quick tempered. She was opinionated. She could be very selfish. A few years ago, Annette began to pray on God's armor. She asked God every day to open her eyes to see life and death and to give her the strength to choose life.

For a while, Annette saw some results. She was nicer, more caring, and more humble. Sadly though, she could still be a mean, arrogant woman with a cutting tongue. After a couple of years, she wondered if this was all the victory she would ever see. She was almost 70 years old. Perhaps the Lord was going to let her die a crotchety old woman.

The more she thought about this, the more it bothered her. She did not want to die with so little fruit of the Spirit in her life. She didn't want to stand barren before Jesus.

For a month, she put her whole heart into the breastplate. She would receive by faith that the Spirit of Sonship was opening her eyes to see life and death, and he was giving her the strength to choose life. As the month went on, she felt a stirring growing in her.

One day, it struck her that she had been putting all of her energy into asking Jesus to show her the death of sin. She noticed that she had placed very little emphasis on asking Jesus to give her the strength to walk in the life he had for her. After a few weeks, her faith began to grow. She believed that Jesus was not done with her.

As her eyes opened to Jesus' life, she found more joy in serving others. Over the next few years, she served in many ministries and saw more growth in her soul.

Then one day, she stumbled upon a friend who had a ministry tutoring underprivileged children. This was a Christian ministry, and the tutors had great freedom to talk about Christ. The friend told Annette that many of their tutors had led entire families to Christ. Something leapt in Annette's heart. She volunteered right away.

That was 10 years ago. Today Annette is almost 80 years old, and she still volunteers 20-30 hours a week. Everyone knows her. She is the kindest, gentlest, most giving woman they have ever met.

Now it is with great joy and faith that Annette puts her breastplate on every day.

9

Free from Trying to Please People

I have been a people-pleaser since early childhood. In high school, I was voted "Most Popular" 2 years in a row. I worked hard to make everyone like me. Walking the school halls, I constantly read people's eyes. How could I make them smile? How could I make them happy?

When I became a pastor, my people-pleasing tendencies went into overdrive. It took me decades to learn that loving people with Jesus' love does not mean always trying to please them.

> ➤ In putting on my breastplate, I first focus on the vertical relationship with my heavenly Father. I receive, in my emotional cup, my heavenly Father's pleasure, acceptance, and approval. I receive open eyes to see life and death, and then I draw from God's strength and desire to walk in life.

> ➤ After this, I am ready to deal with the horizontal subject of how I interact with others.

How much do we try to impress others or earn their approval?

Our relationship with God and our relationships with people are inextricably intertwined. Our Breastplate of Righteousness will not be completely "in place" until we have also asked God to set us free from trying to earn people's approval.

How different would our lives be if we didn't try to impress other people? How many of us would choose different careers, drive different cars, dress differently, act differently, or worship differently? What would change in our emotions? How much time would we save?

Trying to earn other people's approval leaves us exhausted and empty because we can't please everyone. Someone will always find fault with us. We have to constantly increase our effort to achieve our goal of pleasing people.

True freedom from trying to earn people's approval has to begin with being filled with God's approval and his heart to bless.

The Apostle Paul was willing to give up many of his personal rights so that he might win people to Christ. This is the theme of 1 Corinthians 9.

Giving up his personal rights did not mean that Paul was trying to earn people's approval. Paul said, *"I care very little if I am judged by you."* 1 *Corinthians 4:3.* Paul was saying, "I couldn't care less if you want to judge me."

Paul was not callous or abrasive. He was a gentle, humble servant. This verse simply means that he never did anything to try to earn people's approval. He served hungry individuals who wanted to change, as God's Spirit led him.

Because those that are led by the Spirit are sons of God. Romans 8:14

The opposite of trying to earn people's approval is not to be an uncaring, selfish person. It is simply to be a secure servant who blesses others as God's Spirit leads you.

Avoiding critical people

When we allow negative individuals to get inside our hearts, we permit them to rip off the breastplate Jesus died to give us. Some people will constantly judge you, no matter how much you bless and encourage them.

> ➤ I have seen wonderful, successful 50-year-old adults still trying to please a belittling parent.

> ➤ I have seen cheerful, kind, encouraging, single adults foolishly date negative, complaining people.

Permitting those types of individuals to have a deep place in your soul will assure that you will never be able to walk in the fullness of God's delightful, overflowing acceptance of you as his child.

Boundaries = space

When you operate in both the belt and the breastplate, you are a cheerful, caring person and an awesome friend. People will seek you out.

Because your friendship is an uncommon treasure, you don't have to correct people to have proper boundaries. It is more effective to initiate a calm, steady withdrawal and a lessening of the amount of interaction.

The Bible does not tell us to try to have deep relationships with every person. In Romans 12:18 and Hebrews 12:14 we are simply commanded to have peace with every person, as much as possible.

If it is possible, as far as it depends on you, live at peace with everyone.
Romans 12:18

Make every effort to live in peace with all men. Hebrews 12:14

When you graciously pull back and refuse to engage in strife, complaining, negativity, or judging with critical people, you are doing all you can to have peace with them.

Accept one another, then, just as Christ accepted you. Romans 15:7

Romans 15:7 commands us to accept people and think they're wonderful. I regularly counsel individuals to put as much space between themselves and a critical person as is necessary in order to think the other person is wonderful. The breastplate will teach you to be secure about withdrawing from relationships. It is better to have more space and still think someone is wonderful, than to have on-going tension.

The real reason for boundaries… hungry, humble people

I became a Christian at 19 years old. I was the first Christian in my family. Within 18 months, all 5 of my siblings and both of my parents had become Christians.

Although we were all now Christians, my extended family was filled with trouble for 20 more years. My dad constantly created strife and everyone expected me to resolve it. For 20 years, I mediated many 4 to 6 hour intense arguments, caused by my dad's explosions of anger.

After 20 years of mediating, some lines were crossed. My dad attacked my wife and children in ways that I could not permit. I withdrew from him. That season grew into a 6 year period with no interaction.

During those 6 years, my wife, I, and our children all had great peace. Our lives were wonderful, joyful, and fruitful.

In his separate world, my dad's unhappiness increased until he had conflict with every person in his life. When I was not there to act as a buffer, my dad had to face all the consequences of the enmity he generated. His whole world blew up.

Proverbs warns us not to rescue hot-tempered people.

> *A hot-tempered man must pay the penalty;*
> *if you rescue him, you will have to do it again. Proverbs 19:19*

Because I was not there to rescue him, my dad was broken by all the discord in his life. He went to counseling and humbled himself.

In the last decades of his life, he became one of the gentlest, kindest, godliest men I have ever known. He became my inspiration and one of my best friends. At my dad's funeral, I joyfully bragged that he had become my hero. I have never seen any man change as much as my dad changed over the last season of his life.

By constantly putting up with his abuse and being his buffer, I'd held my dad back from the Lord's correction. Once the Lord was able to correct him, without my interference, my dad became the man of God that he was intended to be.

During that 6 year separation, I went to a lot of counseling, and I sought God's voice by his word and his Spirit. The Lord showed me 2 things.

First, he showed me that I had hindered God's work in my dad's life by trying so hard to please him.

Secondly, and more importantly, the Lord showed me that he had hungry, humble people he wanted me to serve. Because I had been so busy trying to please my dad, I hadn't had the time or the emotional energy to help the ones who were humble and ready to change.

That insight broke me.

I will never forget what the Lord said to me in the first few years of my separation from my dad. I was almost 40 years old. I was whining to the Lord about how hard I had tried to help my dad. The Lord gently but firmly told me that I had held my dad back for 20 years.

The Lord's correction of me went further. He told me that every hour I poured into my dad was an hour that he had planned for me to minister to a hungry soul who wanted to change.

In that instant, I could see the thousands of tender people whom I could have helped. I saw 20 years of wasted effort that was needed elsewhere. My soul was tattooed with a deeper understanding that I am not my own. I am given a limited amount of emotional energy. I answer to Jesus for how I spend those reserves. When I expend myself trying to calm people who enjoy drama, I drain my soul trying to bail out the ocean. I waste the gifts Jesus gave me.

Previously, I had always seen boundaries as a hard-hearted response from a self-centered person. I could not have been more wrong.

Through that season, I came to understand that boundaries are a river of love that flows into many streams.

> ➢ For those unwilling to change - I gently withdraw out of love for them.

> ➢ For the hungry - I am available out of love for them.

> ➢ For myself - I experience the joy of being fruitful because of Jesus' love for me.

> *The boundary lines have fallen for me in pleasant places;*
> *surely I have a delightful inheritance. Psalm 16:6*

Tips on drawing boundaries

With a heart that is secure in God's pleasure over you, you are free from trying to please people. You are now ready to offer real help to others, rather than giving in to their demands so they'll like you. You are ready to graciously withdraw from people who demand your help but don't want to change or take responsibility for their own actions.

Here are a few tips:

1. <u>Remember that they are asking for your help. You are not asking for their help!</u>

   Beware of one-way streets! Critical, negative people love to get their feelings hurt. They accuse you of not doing enough for them. Being graciously honest is the limit of your responsibility with most people. Even with senior citizen parents who are critical and negative, you are not required to listen to their criticisms. When you let people take advantage of you and judge you, you are not helping them. It is as if you are booze, and they are alcoholics.

   Keep as much space between yourself and critical people as necessary for you to think they are wonderful.

2. <u>Strategize with them on how they can fix their own problems</u>.

   ➤ They say, "I need money to pay my rent." Your old, people-pleasing self would offer to pay the rent, which doesn't really help them. Now, because you know God is pleased with you, and you want to permanently help the people he sends to you, you can say, "Let's strategize ways you could earn some money. Why don't you go door-to-door offering to mow lawns?"

   ➤ They tell you the same relational problems over and over again. You won't help them by allowing them to complain. Try saying, "You seem to be stuck in a repetitive pattern. May I ask you to read this book, and tell me how it helps you?" Then, ask them about the book every time you see them.

   ➤ They want to tell you about someone who has offended them. You might say, "Let's talk about how you can hear this person's heart and work toward resolution."

When you respond in ways that require the critical, blaming person to own their attitudes and work hard to change, they will become horribly offended and storm off. Let them go! You obeyed Ephesians 4:15. You spoke the truth in love in a way that would help them to grow up and become more like Jesus.

Instead, speaking the truth in love, we will in all things grow up into him who is the Head, that is, Christ. Ephesians 4:15

Strategizing with people on how they can fix their own problems also answers concerns about draining, unsaved relatives. We want to be witnesses of Christ to them. We don't want to cut them off. When they ask for help, we point them to Jesus and gently ask them to take responsibility for their own problems and attitudes.

Strategizing with people on how they can fix their own problems attracts humble people and repels critical, blaming people.

3. Keep thinking about the hungry, humble people.

    With critical, blaming people, you can serve them for one thousand hours, and they don't change at all.

    With humble, hungry people, you can serve them for one hour and their entire lives change.

    Above all, we want to bear the most fruit for Jesus during our short time on this earth.

4. Thank God for caller ID. ☺

Tyrone

Tyrone was not an impressive man.

He was short and a bit overweight. His job was not flashy. As an x-ray technician, Tyrone did the same thing all day, every day. He tried to be nice, but people rarely noticed him.

Tyrone was constantly wearied by the attitudes at his job. They were supposed to be a non-profit hospital, but they drove their employees worse than for-profit companies. He did not believe that he had the strength to do anything about it. He just kept working in the negative atmosphere, as he had for 15 years.

Each day he would drag himself home feeling beat up. Nothing he did was ever good enough. Nothing he did was ever fast enough.

Several years ago, Tyrone began to pray on God's armor. It gave him energy to start the day, but he still felt wiped out and battered by the end of the day. When he prayed on the breastplate, he skimmed over the section on people-pleasing. "After all, that only applies to friends," he thought. One day his wife asked him if he was staying in his current job because he was afraid or because he believed that this was all he deserved. That shook him up!

Tyrone was not one to analyze, but, after his wife's comments, he began to pay more attention to the section on people-pleasing. Over the next 2 years, he slowly implemented some boundaries in his life in regards to what he would put up with at work.

The conditions at his work did not change much, but Tyrone changed. He became more confident. He began to believe that his job was a ministry to people. He began to see the critical people as those who wanted to rip off his breastplate. After 2 years, Tyrone was ready. His wife helped him put together a resume.

To his delight, he had a job offer with a better company within a month. His new job even included a 15% raise. Best of all, the new company had a very positive atmosphere.

Now people remember Tyrone. He is the x-ray tech who obviously cares about them. He is the x-ray tech who gets people to share their stories and who assures them that he will pray for them.

Tyrone is a very impressive man.

Prayers answered immediately

Trying to please people is a chain that Satan wrapped around my soul for decades. Each day that I prayed this aspect of the breastplate, I felt another link break off of that chain.

Transition to the shoes

At this point in the armor, we have won 3 major battles.

1. The belt has set us free from strife.
2. Through the breastplate, we have received our Father's pleasure filling our emotions and setting us free from sin.
3. The breastplate has also set us free from trying to please people and has given us a heart to bless others.

We are now ready for Jesus to help us organize our daily schedule.

We can now ask the Counselor/Comforter to help us put on the 2 shoes of wisdom and peace over every aspect of our daily calendar.

In older versions of the King James Bible, Psalm 37:23 gives the perfect verse to help us transition from the breastplate to the shoes.

The steps of a righteous man are ordered by the Lord. Psalm 37:23 (KJV)

Schedule

=

God's shoes

10

Wisdom and Peace
Guiding my
Daily Schedule

...and having shod your feet with the preparation of the gospel of peace;
Ephesians 6:15 (NAS)

The steps of a man are established by the LORD and he delights in his way.
Psalm 37:23 (NAS)

Feet represent schedule

It is our feet which carry us all day. Jesus said a fascinating thing about feet.

"A person who has had a bath needs only to wash his feet;
his whole body is clean." John 13:10

Jesus taught us that our feet are the body parts that deal directly with a dirty world, literally and figuratively. It is our feet that deal with hectic schedules, traffic, lack of sleep, interruptions, and bills.

For all these dirty, worldly steps that our feet deal with in our daily schedules, God provides shoes.

My story about schedule

For the first 20 years of my life, I believed that if I worked harder, then I would be more productive. In my college years, I worked for my dad's electrical company during the summer months. It was excellent money, and I loved the hard work. My second summer, I progressed from the level of helper to journeyman electrician. I took great pride in outworking every other person on the job.

In my dad's company, there was one particular job foreman, Danny Waters, who had the reputation of being the most effective job boss.

Halfway through my second summer, I was transferred to a site where Danny was running the project. I was so excited to finally meet and work under the famous Danny Waters! I pictured him as an intense, high speed drill sergeant. I thrilled at the idea that he would challenge me by requiring a breakneck pace.

My first day working for Danny was a major disappointment. Rather than a drill sergeant, I discovered that he was a slow-talking, friendly country boy. At 7 a.m., he didn't bark out orders.

Instead, he called all his journeymen and master electricians together for a morning "chat" over a cup of coffee. When this chat stretched beyond 20 minutes, I was appalled at the waste of time. Even though it was my first day on Danny's job, I requested to be excused from the meeting when restlessness overcame me. I asked him if I could take one of the helpers and get started on the floor that was my responsibility. I assured Danny that I had studied the plans and was ready to work.

After he dismissed me, my helper and I dove in. I felt a combination of disappointment and smugness. I was let down that the great Danny Waters was so slow. I arrogantly assumed that I would easily out-perform everyone in his pitiful crew.

The first day, I was shocked to find out that my floor accomplished less than any of the other floors. I attributed that to first-day adjustments and to a lack of familiarity with the job.

The second day, I totally skipped the morning "chat." I literally ran all day. I worked my helper at a torrid pace. I can't describe my shock and dismay when my floor again achieved less than the others.

Through that experience, I discovered that being prepared to be productive is more than just working hard. In those morning chats, Danny carefully made sure everyone was operating in wisdom. He patiently talked through each person's daily goals. He dissected the man hours and materials needed for each situation. He analyzed what the plumbers, carpenters, and HVAC men would be doing and how we could best co-ordinate our efforts with theirs.

After their morning chat with Danny, the other electricians didn't have one-tenth as many obstacles, mistakes, and interruptions as I did. Danny Waters taught me that working smart will out-produce blind effort every day. Danny taught me the value of taking time to get prepared so that I could have an effective day. I learned to humbly, patiently, and attentively attach great importance to my morning chats with my job foreman!

This third piece of armor begins with a humble, patient, attentive chat with our job foreman, who is also our heavenly Father.

Nearly every activity on our schedule is birthed out of a motivation to be productive. The reason we involve our children in ballet, school, soccer, or band is so we can be productive parents who raise productive children. Cleaning the house, going to church, going to work, and buying Christmas presents are all attempts to be productive.

Sometimes, however, our schedules control us more than we control them. We can over-commit or miss great opportunities.

This third piece of armor allows us to maximize both our schedule and our level of peace.

Praying on God's shoes involves examining all the hectic pieces of our daily schedule and asking 2 questions about each section of our day. Do I have wisdom? Do I have peace?

Counselor / Comforter – Shoes of Wisdom and Peace

In his final message to his disciples before the cross, Jesus spoke extensively about the Holy Spirit. In the New International Version (1984), Jesus calls the Holy Spirit the "Counselor" 4 times: John 14:16 & 26, 15:26, and 16:7. In the King James Version, these same 4 passages use the word "Comforter."

In the original Greek, this is the word "paráklētos," which means to "*walk beside*." A paráklētos is someone who gives both counsel and comfort; therefore, both translations are correct. The Holy Spirit is our paráklētos who walks beside us, counseling us with wisdom and comforting us with peace.

Am I operating in wisdom in this aspect of my schedule?

The 8th word in, *And having shod your feet with the preparation of the gospel of peace Eph. 6:15 (NAS)* is the word "preparation." I ask the Counselor if I am "prepared," through his wisdom, for the upcoming responsibilities of my day.

This is a dynamic and engaging question. When I lay out a specific goal and ask for wisdom, I have 5 questions that automatically scroll through my mind.
1. Do I have the emotional and physical energy for this task?
2. Is this a high priority?
3. Do I have enough time set aside if things don't go well?
4. What possible disruptions could happen?
5. Have I gathered all necessary resources?

Am I peaceful about this aspect of my schedule?

The last word of Ephesians 6:15 is the beautiful word "peace." The Comforter wants us to wear shoes that are comfortable. With this shoe, I ask the Holy Spirit to search my heart to see if I have peace about each of the particular objectives I have set for my day.

Wisdom is the energizing side of my soul. Peace is the calming side of my soul. Wisdom tends to involve logic. Peace tends to be more of an emotionally intuitive experience.

Many times wisdom and peace both come quickly. However, I am consistently surprised when I find a "pause" in my heart related to either wisdom or peace, in regards to a planned point in my schedule. These delightful interruptions give me great confidence that I am receiving specific direction from my heavenly Father.

Balance

Our feet are the main reason that we are able to maintain our physical balance. Feet are marvelous medical specimens. The human foot contains 28 bones, 112 ligaments, and 20 muscles. The intricacy of this design is so amazing that we can run, climb stairs, jump, and walk without falling on our faces. Feet keep us balanced.

The greatest reason feet are able to keep us balanced is because we have 2 of them. We are not monopod beings. We are bipeds. Having 2 feet enables us to tackle almost any terrain and maintain our balance. In the same way, if we have equal amounts of wisdom and peace in our daily schedule, we are balanced and will walk through our day with productivity and rest.

If I sense the Lord's direction 20 times in an hour-long prayer session, half of them will be impressions about something in my schedule. I either sense a lack of wisdom or a lack of peace about some upcoming activity. During these times, I ask the Lord to patiently sort out this upcoming agenda until I am clear.

In 10 minutes of putting on God's shoes, I can avoid hours of delays or wrong turns in my calendar.

Here are some tips that have helped me when praying on God's shoes.

Tips

1. <u>Be ready for the Holy Spirit to remove some things from our schedule.</u>

   We can almost feel the Lord smiling at us when we bring our schedule to him. We try to do too much! Without prayer, we foolishly believe that we will have everything on our long list done in one day. The Holy Spirit enjoys gently removing things from our daily plans. He enjoys giving us peaceful productivity.

2. <u>Don't forget to pray over our evenings.</u>

   Evenings are when we are worn out, stressed out, and grumpy. Amazingly, most people forget to pray over their evenings. We put great energy and focus into our workday, and we crash in the evenings. It's no wonder that the worst family arguments occur in the evenings.

   If we don't pray on our shoes for our evenings, we won't be wise or peaceful at the end of the day. The Lord wants to speak to us in great detail about our evenings. Our family time is very important to Jesus.

3. <u>Pray over our eating and exercise habits.</u>

   I think that I am going to work out every day this week. Then I put on the shoes, and the Lord smiles. Soon, I have the wisdom and peace to have 3 to 4 workouts this week.

   I think that am going to eat great this week and lose 5 pounds. Then I put on the shoes, and the Lord smiles. Soon I have the wisdom and peace to be consistent in my eating without trying to be dramatic.

I've made thousands of adjustments in these 2 areas in the past 25 years. In each case, the idea for the adjustment came while putting on my shoes. I've been able to change my habits with the changing seasons in my life. With wisdom and peace, we can take small steps that help us pace our eating and exercising.

4. Pray over the direction of our lives.

What will my life look like this time next year? Do I want to stay in this house for 10 more years? Is it time to talk with my kids about college? How will I handle my parents aging?

With the shoes, the Lord often gives us time to look forward in our walk. Praying for wisdom and peace over the direction of our lives brings short term and long term rest.

5. Always have a pen and paper or a phone recorder available.

The shoes are the pieces of the armor where the Lord often gives us many ideas. When we ask the Lord these questions, he often re-arranges our schedules and reminds us of things we have forgotten. Having a pen and paper handy allows us to remember every point, stay organized, and keep on praying.

Reggie

Reggie comes around the curve on the interstate and traffic slows to a crawl. "It looks like it is going to be a long commute," Reggie says to himself. "This is perfect. This is just what I need today."

Reggie is not being sarcastic. Since Reggie doesn't have to be at work until 9 a.m., and he leaves for work at 7 a.m., he is always relaxed about his commute time. In light traffic, it takes 45 minutes, but, in heavy traffic, it takes an hour or more. Today looks like a heavy traffic day. However, with his mega coffee, instrumental worship music, and rich prayer life, Reggie's car is a place of peace.

Better yet, Reggie has just arrived at his favorite piece of the armor. He is putting on his shoes. With a busy day planned, Reggie is glad to have the extra drive time to pray on his shoes.

"Today looks like an extra hectic day, Lord. We have only one week left to finish that order for the Feldstein account." Immediately, Reggie remembers that he needs to check on the supply of tin he has on backorder. Reggie is the operations manager of a small manufacturing firm, and he loves his job, even with thousands of daily hang-ups. Thinking about the backorder of tin, Reggie grabs his phone. It is always set on mute for incoming calls and is in record mode when he is praying. Reggie records a message reminding himself to call on the tin backorder as soon as he gets to the office. As Reggie continues to ask for God's wisdom on this tin order, he senses that he might need to switch suppliers.

He might even need to see if he can get an emergency order from another company. Grabbing his phone again, Reggie leaves himself a note to ask Jevon to contact the other supply company and place a second order. "It won't hurt us to have a double supply of tin. We always use it."

Reggie thanks God for Jevon! He has been a Godsend as an assistant. "Yikes, Lord, I forgot to ask Jevon how his mother's surgery went yesterday." Reggie grabs the phone recorder again to remind himself to send Jevon an email about his mom, as soon as he gets to the office.

Reggie chuckles as he thinks about how his team teases him about his long lists at their 9 a.m. briefing each morning. "They didn't mind the bonuses last year, though," Reggie says with a smile.

"Okay, Lord, back to the order for the Feldstein account."

Fifteen minutes and 8 more phone notes later, Reggie is ready to think about his lunch chat with his wife, Diane. She works hard as a nurse in the mother-baby unit at Kennestone Hospital. Yesterday was her second day in a row of her 3 weekly 12 hour shifts.

Thankfully, she has the next 2 days off. She will be tired today, but she will be eager to chat by lunchtime. When she is off, Reggie always brings his PB&J sandwich and an apple so he can have lunch while catching up with her on the phone.

As Reggie begins to pray about his upcoming conversation with Diane, he remembers that his daughter, Eliana, has another JV basketball game tonight at 7 p.m. Either Reggie or Diane tries to make every game, but tonight maybe they both can make it. As Reggie prays about this, he doesn't sense wisdom. "Okay Lord, that is not realistic." As he prays for more wisdom, he remembers that his son, Tim, is still struggling in vocabulary and geography. "Lord, can you please show me some wisdom for tonight?" His mind drifts through different possibilities when a thought hits him. "Diane has missed Eliana's last 2 games and will want to go. Tim and I both love watching the Braves baseball games. Maybe Tim and I could watch the game together on TV. We could mute the commercials to work on schoolwork. This could be his reward if he gets all his other homework done by 7 p.m."

Reggie smiles and feels great peace about this idea. He grabs his phone and adds this thought to their lunch chat agenda.

"Traffic is really slow today, Lord. Do you have anything extra for Diane and I to discuss?" As Reggie prays about their marriage, he thinks about that class at their church on ministering to visitors. Reggie spends some time asking the Lord about that opportunity. The more he prays about that class, the less peace he feels. He asks for wisdom. They are already small-group leaders, and this class feels like too much. Diane loves greeting visitors, though.

"How about it Lord? Doing both feels stressful." As he prays for wisdom and peace, a thought pops into Reggie's head, "Is it time to consider stepping down as small-group leaders?" "Is that you, Lord," Reggie says out loud. "We have been small-group leaders for

3 years and we like it, but we both feel called to minister to visitors."

As Reggie continues to pray, he doesn't sense anything else from the Lord. He realizes that Jesus is done talking to him on this subject. That always means that Jesus wants him to talk with Diane about this new idea. He grabs his phone and adds this item to his "Diane phone chat" list. He grins as he thinks of Diane's excitement. She loves it when he brings suggestions to her early in the process. It is going to be a great phone talk today. "Happy wife, happy life!"

"Okay, Lord, let's move on to this afternoon. This Feldstein order is pressuring all of us. Our afternoons tend to be scattered, and we all get frustrated. Is this a day when we need a second team meeting at 1 p.m.?" The more Reggie prays about this, the more peace he feels. His team needs some massaging. They are a bit frazzled. As his mind drifts to the afternoon strategy time, he keeps coming back to the weariness of his team. "Lord, are you telling me to bless them with something extra today?"

Reggie feels peace about looking for an idea to reward his team, but he doesn't feel wisdom about the timing. "Lord, should I just talk to the boss today about finding a reward for next week, when the order is done?" Peace and wisdom both fit perfectly with that idea. Reggie smiles as he remembers the last reward outing he and the boss cooked up. He grabs the phone and rattles off 3 different ideas to run by the boss of rewards for his team.

As Reggie scans the rest of his day, he senses that he is done putting on his shoes. He feels so confident about the Lord's specific direction in his life for this day. It will now be easy to take up the Shield of Faith and release God's favor on his life.

Tension in our homes

In families with 2 or more children, so much of the tension comes because of hectic schedules. Households are trying to do too much, and they are having trouble communicating. These overloaded, poorly communicated schedules are the reason for much tension in a busy home.

If we pray on our shoes in the morning, our homes will be filled with great peace.

One good hour of prayer will save you 5 hours of mistakes, frustration, tension, misunderstandings, and wasted effort.

Prayers answered immediately

This weapon is the easiest.

We all get instant responses when we ask God to give us wisdom and peace over each part of our day. Hearing multiple points of direction from God about our schedule increases our faith. After we put on our shoes, our faith is very high.

Perhaps this is why Paul chose the Shield of Faith to follow the Shoes of Wisdom and Peace.

Favor
=
Shield

11

Understanding
God's Favor

*...Above all, taking the shield of faith
with which you will be able to quench all the fiery darts of the wicked one.*
Ephesians 6:16 (NKJV)

Faith is high – prayers are short

Paul very intentionally positioned the shield as the 4th piece of armor. By the time we have seen God move in the first 3 pieces of armor, our faith is extremely high. Picking up the Shield of Faith is a time of releasing God's favor in different areas of our lives.

It may take me 30 to 60 minutes to put on the first 3 pieces of armor, but the 4th piece, the Shield of Faith, only takes me a few minutes. By this time, I am strong.

I pick 5 to 10 specific subjects in my life where I am asking for God's favor. I make my declarations of faith quickly and confidently. My standard statements of faith are generally, *"I trust you for…"* or *"I receive…"*

There are occasions where the Lord will place on me an extra burden of intercession for an individual or situation. In those cases, I will soak that subject in faith, in the Lord's presence, for hours, days, or weeks, until I sense the Lord's release. This tends to be the exception. Most of the time, I make all of my declarations in a few minutes and move onto the helmet.

"Above all" - Faith is really important to God

For many years, I was a spiritual pauper. I hoped that God would feel sorry for me. I hoped that my saying "please" 500 times would make a difference. The Shield of Faith forced me to face my beggarly attitude.

If you are not comfortable with asking God to bless you, Appendix A may help you. Appendix A is the story of how I came to understand God's favor through in-depth Bible studies.

When I say, "I trust you to…" or "I receive…," I immediately know that God is pleased that I trust him.

And without faith it is impossible to please God,
because anyone who comes to him must believe that he exists
and that he rewards those who earnestly seek him. Hebrews 11:6

"Take up" = Be aggressive

With the breastplate, we are still and patient as the Holy Spirit, our armor bearer, carefully fits God's breastplate over our hearts.

With the shield, though, it is almost the opposite. Paul gives us a specific admonition to be aggressive and "take up" faith.

The Greek word for "take up" is "analambanō." In a Greek dictionary, the first expanded definition of "analambanō" is "to take and then to be amazed at what you have received." That definition gives me chills. What an awesome word! I have experienced this aspect of taking up faith and then being amazed thousands of times in my life.

The command to "take up" the shield teaches me 2 things about faith.

1. Faith is not something God will hand to us.

    We can sit and cry all day, "God, where are you?" God will not feel so sorry for us. He will not shove faith into our hands. God will wait until we choose to say, "I trust you that…" Sadly, there are some people who have spent an entire lifetime crying out for God's help, yet have never chosen to "take up" faith.

2. Faith is not something God resists letting you have.

    God is not your enemy. When you reach out to take faith, He does not violently resist you. The implication of the Greek word "analambanō" is that the instant you reach out to take faith, God quickly hands it to you.

This is why faith is so intimately linked to sensing the presence of God.

Faith does more than overcome emotions. When we open our mouths and declare our verbal trust in God, it forcefully re-directs our emotions and requires them to line up with God's promises.

➢   In countless places of irritation, I would declare aloud, "I trust you to give me a desire to understand this person's emotional perspective." Instantly, God's amazing eagerness would fill me with a curious hunger to listen and learn.

➢   So often, in emotional anguish, I would speak the words, "I trust you to give me peace and calmness." Each time I said those words, I would feel increasing levels of peace and calmness filling my emotions. It was always amazing.

➢   Overwhelmed by emotions of confusion, I would say, "I trust you to show me wisdom." I would then be amazed at how the Lord would begin to show me one step at a time.

God desires to make his presence very real and tangible in our emotions. When we tap into the faith currency of Heaven, we gain the benefits of Heaven.

My specific faith prayers

In younger years, I often trusted God for finances, health, and favor over my children and marriage. I may still pray those prayers at times.

In the last 10 years, though, I find myself praying deeper, stronger faith prayers. I find myself praying subjects of more profound faith and using the stronger phrase, *"I claim!,"* I find that my faith has grown and strengthened after years of taking up my shield.

When I use the phrase, *"I claim!"* I take up my shield on the truly important issues of faith. I pray things such as:

- ➢ I claim a humble, passionate heart for you all the days of my life.
- ➢ I claim the privilege of being fruitful for your kingdom.
- ➢ I claim a hunger for your word.
- ➢ I claim rivers of your truth, righteousness, wisdom, and peace flowing through me.
- ➢ I claim that your love for your people and for the lost will flood my soul.

Ken

Ken never believed in prayer.

He rarely admitted that to others. He just saw so many Christians praying so many things and could not think of one instance when he was sure that the result was because of an answered prayer.

Ken truly loved Jesus and followed him. He just didn't believe that prayer made that much difference. He believed that God was going to work out his plan whether Ken prayed or not. He realized that he was stale in his walk with Jesus, but he didn't know how to fix the problem.

The day that Ken read about praying on God's armor, his life changed forever. His deepest thirst was satisfied when he learned that there are some prayers God answers immediately. He quickly understood the concept. He realized that each piece of armor involves us asking God to give us part of his heart.

Ken now loves praying on the armor.

He knows that God has changed him and guided him hundreds of times through putting on the belt, breastplate, and shoes.

Perhaps the sweetest piece of armor for Ken is the Shield of Faith.

Ken used to think that intercession was the only kind of prayer. Once he realized that intercession is the fourth piece of armor, he began to love the very thing he used to despise.

Ken is a lawyer. He understands contracts in detail. Thus, he understands that the words "I trust you" mean that he can ask and rest in God's ultimate wisdom and power.

Ken now likes asking God to do amazing things. Better yet, he has seen God do some wonderful things that are beyond logic.

Ken is a powerful man of prayer. Ken is a man of faith.

Prayers answered immediately

Ken is one of my favorite people. I often wonder how many others have felt the same as Ken, but they were not bold enough to say it aloud. I remember being stunned and delighted when he told me that he did not pray because he never saw answers to his prayers. I was thrilled by Ken's challenge. I asked him to study through this book. It is now such a joy today to see how much Ken loves prayer.

The shield transitioning to the helmet

How appropriate to be full of faith as we now move on to the 5th piece of armor and deal with the subject of our thoughts and our eternal salvation as we put on the Helmet of Salvation.

Thoughts
=
Helmet

12

Thought Life
and Confidence
in Heaven

Take the helmet of salvation Ephesians 6:17

Fear and lust

The Helmet of Salvation covers our minds.

In our thought lives, the first 4 pieces of the armor win ordinary mental battles.

1. Anger is completely resolved by the belt.
2. Shame and rejection are healed by the breastplate.
3. Schedule stress is calmed by the shoes.
4. Doubts are rinsed away by the shield.

Fear and lust, however, are 2 vicious attacks that can bypass the first 4 weapons and leave a person mentally crippled.

Such thoughts pound on our minds like jackhammers in overdrive. Normal thoughts are easily controlled and re-directed. Obsessive thoughts overwhelm and consume us.

Fear

No matter what fear we are battling, the single thought that goes through our minds, when afraid, are the 2 words, *"avoid pain."* All fear is connected to the passion to escape pain. At some point we either faced the possibility of, or experienced, being embarrassed, rejected, exposed, or harmed.

Every person has some rational fears. Rational fears can be God's warning to avoid dangerous situations.

The difference with obsessive fears is that they are irrational. A person with obsessive fears is unable to reason. All logic is thrown out the window. All levelheaded considerations are shut down.

With obsessive fears, our imagination locks onto the possibility of pain and begins to expand on the idea in our brains. The thought of facing this pain paralyzes us. Obsessive fears drive us to extremely unwise behaviors. I have seen mothers, who fear their child being molested, spend hours each day scouring the internet for horror stories of child molestation. When asked to consider the foolishness of feeding irrational fears, these mothers respond with an almost demonically vicious overreaction.

Obsessive fears have a wide range. People can fear loneliness, bodily injury, heights, crowds, harm coming to their children, or failure in business.

Lust

When driven by lust, the controlling thought that dominates our minds 1,000 times per minute is the phrase, *"I want that."*

The most common direction of lust is toward sexually immorality. Lust, however, is also the root in people who are consumed with drugs, materialism, selfish ambition, pride, or greed.

Feeling Helpless

Obsessive thoughts grab our brains and laugh at us. They tell us that we are helpless to control our own minds and that we must obey them. Nights are the hardest time for most people who battle obsessive thoughts of fear or lust.

My battle with lust

When I became a Christian, I had already completed 2 years of college as a non-Christian. Unfortunately, I had fed myself a lot of filth and immorality before I gave my life to Jesus. If my mind wanted to obsess on lusting after sexually immoral thoughts, it had an abundance of stored up pictures and memories upon which to draw.

For 4 years after I became a Christian, I had wars with lust that were horribly discouraging. I passionately wanted to follow Jesus Christ in every area of my life, and I saw God's blessing on my life. I was in full-time ministry, yet this miserable clash raged in my mind. I was so weary of feeling filthy, repenting, and asking God to set me free. I guarded my eyes. I did not watch TV. I did not look lustfully at any lady. I prayed constantly, studied God's word, fasted, and sought accountability and counseling. I could maintain a marginal victory during the day.

At night, though, I would lie in bed with a tired body and a mind that wouldn't stop thinking. I didn't know how to get my mind to be quiet when I was physically tired and unable to sleep. My prayers felt like I was shooting a squirt gun onto a large campfire. I felt like I was being mugged by 10 strong men.

I sought counsel, and I sought God. The only answer that people gave me was that this would always be a weak area, especially for a single man. I could not find any person who believed that a single man could ever have complete victory in this area. It was as if the promise of God's armor, "be strong," did not apply to lust.

Then one day in the fall of 1981...

I went to a one-day ministers' seminar. By this time, I was on staff at a great church in Birmingham, Alabama. The seminar was inspiring. The speaker gave fascinating and motivating teachings. It was also stirring to sit in a civic center with 2,000 other pastors.

Halfway through the day, the speaker taught on Romans 6. He challenged us, as leaders in God's church, to lead the way in being strong in God's word. He asked how many of us full-time ministers would commit over the next year to memorizing Romans 6. In my enthusiastic and vulnerable state, I raised my hand up into the air along with about 1,000 other men.

The instant I put my hand in the air, I realized the enormity of my commitment. My next thought was, "Oh, you stupid idiot!"

I didn't know anyone who memorized whole chapters of scripture. As a baby Christian, I tried once to memorize the entire 48 verses of Matthew 5. It was a terrible failure! The first 10 verses were delicious. The second 10 verses were good. The third 10 verses were hard. The fourth 10 verses were like eating dry dust! Finally, the last 8 verses were like eating dry dust embedded with slivers of glass on a nauseous stomach. I forced verses 41-48 into my mind in about an hour, said them once, and then vomited up the entire idea of ever again memorizing a chapter of God's word.

These were the emotions that flooded back as I stared at my rebellious hand in the air. I was feeling very, very stupid.

Time froze in that moment. Hating myself for my impulsiveness, I made a life-changing decision.

I said to myself, "Okay, I'm stuck! My word is the essence of my integrity. I have to keep this commitment, but I'm going to take my time. I'm going to take the entire year of 1982 to memorize this chapter. I'm going to do the slowest memorization in history."

Super slow memorizing

I resolved to spend a maximum of 5 minutes a day on memorizing. I made it the first part of my prayer time.

I flaunted the fact that I was taking my time. I didn't see any purpose or benefit in memorizing these 23 verses, other than to keep my commitment.

During those 5 minutes, if I felt pushed or stuffed at all, I would stay at the same place and not even think about adding new verses for a few weeks. I enjoyed quoting the verses I had already learned, but I refused to add new verses quickly.

By the end of March, I had the first 9 verses memorized. I knew them so well that they were easy. However, I was fiercely determined to not move onto verse 10.

I was going too fast! 9 verses in 3 months was a faster pace than I had intended. I was resolute to take the entire year. I wanted to teach myself a lesson to avoid impulsive decisions in the future.

Reverse order quoting

I now knew the first 9 verses so well that I felt bored with quoting them. I began to play a game to relieve the boredom. If I was not going to add verse 10 yet, perhaps I could switch up the order of my quoting. Instead of quoting in a forward order of verses 1 through 9, I would begin with verse 9 and try to quote in reverse order.

This felt like fun. It also enabled me to move more slowly through the quoting, which was my goal. By quoting in reverse order, I was able to delay adding verse 10 for another month and not be bored.

Quoting in reverse order seemed to add richness to my 5 minutes. In reverse order, each verse felt like a unique, special, and individual friend, and in forward order they felt like a unified, powerful family.

Again, I still saw no major spiritual benefit to this daily regimen. I grudgingly admitted that it did seem to make it easier to pray. My main goal, however, was to move slowly as a way to punish myself for a foolish commitment.

May 1982 - A dream that changed my life

I'd often had ghastly dreams in which I saw Satan attack me. Usually, in those dreams, my mouth would freeze, and I could not form the word, "Jesus." I would wake up in a terrified, cold sweat.

This dream, however, was different.

In this dream, we were at a retreat center with my youth group. Satan was coming out of the mountain, throwing lightning bolts and bringing storm clouds. With each step he took, every living thing died in his wake. Trees withered, water evaporated, animals turned to skeletons and darkness ruled. He was looking directly at me, screaming angrily that he was going to destroy every teen in my youth group. As their youth pastor, I knew it was my job to protect them.

As Satan came closer, I was shocked to find that I was not afraid. In the dream, I started quoting Romans 6 at him. The words poured out of my mouth like a sonic shock wave of God's power. Verse after verse flowed out without conscience thought. Satan was overwhelmed as I stood quoting. He withered before me and blew away in the dust. The skies cleared, all life was restored, and I felt God's love pour through the sunshine onto me.

I woke up stunned. I knew that God had spoken powerfully to me in that dream. I could no longer pretend that my quoting was a grudging commitment. I had fallen in love with Romans 6.

Even more, I realized that I had discovered an untapped power in being able to quote an extensive passage of God's word in forward order and reverse order. I had been feeling this power for months, but I was afraid to admit it. When I quoted God's word out loud, I felt calm, clear, and strong.

It confused me because it was so easy. I never sweated or strained. My memorizing felt like having a delightful dinner of laughter and love with dear friends.

I knew these verses better than I knew my own name. Because I had gone so slowly, I had put my heart into this passage. I ate God's word. I chewed the meat of God's word slowly, and it was delicious. The words of Romans 6 made a lot of sense to me. They captivated my heart and filled my mind.

Somehow, without strain or effort, I had been given God's most powerful weapon that exists on the earth for Christians.

Conquering lust

I began applying this newfound weapon to my battles with lust. When I was lying in bed trying to go to sleep, and my mind began to wander into lustful thoughts, I actively engaged my mind in quoting Romans 6. Sometimes I quoted forward, but, in the more intense battles, I found greater power if I quoted in reverse order.

To say that I was absolutely astounded would be the understatement of the century! I began to be excited about battling lust. I eagerly watched for any attempt by Satan to distract me with a lustful thought. When it came, I would gleefully pound it to dust by quoting Romans 6.

Within one month, I had 100% control over my thought life. After 4 years of total failure, I had found freedom. I have maintained this wonderful victory from that time forward.

It was like going from being a baseball player who struck out every time to one who hits a home run every time. The change was so dramatic that I was stunned beyond words.

I had stumbled upon the greatest revelation I have ever learned about memorizing chapters of the Bible.

Hunger-based memorization

Because I only memorized when I was very, very hungry for another verse, I never felt in a hurry. I was not trying to impress God or people.

33 years later, I still memorize this way. I have 42 chapters that I quote every week. I still do not permit myself to memorize more than a chapter a year, unless they are very short chapters or I am in an extensive fasting season.

Sometimes, I quote from the first to the last verse. Other times, I quote from the last to the first verse. Quoting a chapter in reverse order engages my brain more deeply than quoting forward.

I have never tried to be impressive. I don't like telling people that I have memorized so many chapters. I quote all of my chapters every week in prayer, and I only memorize new verses when I am very hungry. I move as slowly as I possibly can in memorizing.

Here are 2 things that I have learned from this mind-blowing discovery.

1. **It is foolish to tell your mind to stop thinking about something.**

    All of those years when I battled obsessive, lustful thoughts, I vigorously ordered my mind, "Stop thinking that!"

    Telling our minds to "stop thinking that" is like blowing air on a fire. If it's a very small fire, it puts the fire out. However, if the fire has any strength at all, then blowing the air increases the flames.

    You can't imagine how exhausted you become trying to put out the flames of obsessive thoughts by blowing the air of "stop thinking that" on them.

On second thought, maybe you do know how exhausting that is. Maybe you have had your own battles with the obsessive thoughts of fear or lust.

The key to victory is to actively engage our minds in something more powerful than the temptation! After 5 minutes of quoting Romans 6, my mind was completely calm, clear, alert, peaceful and under my control. The flame of lust was extinguished. It wasn't even a battle.

I had previously tried quoting single verses when battling lust. Quoting a few single verses was like shooting a squirt gun into a campfire. When I actively engaged my mind and heart into an entire chapter of God's word, it was like directing water from a fireman's hose onto the campfire. Quoting verses in reverse order engages the mind even more. When I had a big fire, I would quote in reverse order.

I became drunk with this newfound power. For a month or 2, I was thrilled when a lustful thought would attack me so I could turn on my fireman's hose and drown that spark. I was a 24-year old, single man who had complete, joyous, and total victory over lust. God's word became an impenetrable protection over my mind. God's word became my helmet.

That was over 33 years ago, and the victory has remained just as total, joyous, and sweet every day since then.

2. This power is what the Bible calls "meditation" on God's word.

In Joshua 1, Psalm 1, and Psalm 119, some wonderful, powerful promises are made to the person who meditates on God's word. These promises are not available to us unless we meet the Biblical definition of "meditation."

One of the most important laws in interpreting the Bible is to understand words in the context and framework in which the author understood them.

When Joshua and David commanded us to meditate on God's word, what did they mean by the word "meditate"?
How much printed material was available in their day? Could they pick up their copy of the Bible that they carried around with them to meditate on God's word? Tradition tells us that Levitical students in Paul's day were expected to memorize the entire Old Testament by the time they were 12 years old.

In almost every New Testament letter that Paul wrote, he referenced specific, detailed passages from the Old Testament. How do you think Paul was able to reference those passages? Did he look them up in a concordance and then read them out of one of the 15 copies of the Old Testament that he kept handy? Printed material was not available. Paul referenced these verses from memory. He could quote the entire Old Testament.

Again, what did Joshua and David mean by the word "meditate?" They were referring to quoting long passages (whole chapters and books) of scripture while thinking about how they apply to our lives.

Do not let this Book of the Law depart from your mouth;
meditate on it day and night, so that you may be careful to do
everything written in it. Then you will be prosperous and successful. Joshua 1:8

This new discovery of great power that I made at 24 years old was something that had been in the scriptures for over 3,000 years. I discovered how to set my mind on things above.

"Set your minds on things above." Colossians 3:2

I discovered how to

"…take captive every thought to make it obedient to Christ."
2 Corinthians 10:5

Paul and other Torah students memorized 929 chapters in 7 years, between the ages of 5 and 12.

An average person can memorize a chapter of God's word in a month with only 10 minutes a day of effort.

I have memorized 42 chapters in 33 years. That is a very slow pace. I take my time, and I enjoy memorizing. I never rush through a chapter. I spend weeks on one verse, and I do not move forward until I am deliciously hungry for the next verse.

> ➤ I quote when I am exercising.
> ➤ I quote every night to be able to fall asleep quickly.
> ➤ I quote when driving.
> ➤ When I pray on the armor of God, I usually quote a chapter between each piece of the armor. This makes my prayer time even richer and sweeter.
> ➤ Whenever I am overwrought or battling any negative emotion, I quote.

Quoting aloud instantly releases God's power into my mind. It is so heavenly to have control over my thought life.

Jogging in place

This morning my wife, Beth, chuckled as she walked by me. She grinned and said to me, "I hope I have a grandson with my husband's entertaining personality." My wife was tickled because I was jogging in place while loudly quoting verses. I still only permit myself 5 minutes to quote verses from a new chapter. When I prepare to work out, I jog in place for 5 minutes while quoting aloud my new verses. Then I begin my stretching.

Currently, I am almost done with II Timothy 4. I have been memorizing II Timothy for 3 years. This morning I quoted II Timothy 4:14, then 4:13, then 4:12, then 4:11, then 4:10, and then 4:9. After that, I quoted II Timothy 4:1-8 in forward order. Because

I only permit myself 5 minutes to work on new verses, memorization never becomes drudgery. It is my favorite time of the day.

Will this weapon become a part of your life?

In our church we have over 100 adults who memorize a chapter of God's word every year. This is only about 5% of the adults in our church, not a high percentage. I have discovered that there are 2 main reasons why others do not enjoy this weapon as much as I do.

1. Many people do not battle obsessive thoughts as much as I do.

    I have an obsessive brain. My brain goes at full speed all the time. I have quoted God's word to help me fall asleep almost every night for over 30 years. When I wake up in the middle of the night, quoting enables me to calm my mind and go back to sleep. If you have problems sleeping, quoting God's word is the perfect tonic. I can usually fall back to sleep in a few minutes.

2. Most people hurry through memorization and don't understand the sweetness of hunger-based memorizing.

    By never spending more than 5 minutes working on a new verse on any day, I am always eager for the next day. I never move on to another verse until I am very hungry. I usually spend between 2 and 4 weeks on one verse. Memorizing is not a matter of intelligence. It is only a matter of hunger. I never feel pressure. It is always sweet.

    Memorizing a new verse is like eating a steak. The slower you chew the more you enjoy it. Most people memorize as though they had to eat a 16 ounce steak in 2 minutes.

    Memorizing a new verse is like adopting a new child. Each child is unique and deserves special attention. Most people cram in order to memorize as though they are adopting a new child every 2 days. They get overwhelmed, and they don't take the time to get to know each child.

My actual prayer time over the Helmet of Salvation is short. Since I quote a chapter between each piece of armor, I have a calm mind. My main goal when praying on the Helmet of Salvation is to speak out loud my confidence that I am going to Heaven.

Reasons for confidence in Heaven

The most powerful reason for having confidence in going to Heaven is because God's word promises us eternal life. Here are my 3 favorite verses on being confident that I am going to Heaven:

I write these things to you who believe in the name of the Son of God so that you may know that you have eternal life. I John 5:13

Those who have served well gain an excellent standing and great assurance in their faith in Christ Jesus. 1 Timothy 3:13

Therefore, my brothers, be all the more eager to make your calling and election sure. For if you do these things, you will never fall, [11] and you will receive a rich welcome into the eternal kingdom of our Lord and Savior Jesus Christ.
2 Peter 1:10-11

When I pray on the Helmet of Salvation, I declare out loud that I live only for Jesus and that I trust Jesus' blood and Jesus' righteousness to bring me to Heaven.

The other reason for having confidence in going to Heaven is because we have seen Jesus change us. Many people trust the scriptures, but they worry that they somehow haven't done things right. They worry that they may have misunderstood what it means to be a Christian. That is why the fruit of a changed life is a powerful point of confidence in our eternal salvation.

I personally think that this is why the Helmet of Salvation is the fifth piece of armor. By the time the Holy Spirit clothes us in the first 4 pieces of armor, we have seen many immediate answers to prayer. We know that God has given us more of his heart. We know that we are changed.

Dear friends, if our hearts do not condemn us, we have confidence before God
I John 3:21

Millie

Millie had a deep, dark, private secret. Millie was obsessed with fear. She had shared her fears with friends many times. They all seemed to trust so much more easily than she did. Eventually, they appeared to grow tired of Millie's fears, so she began to hide them and pretend everything was fine with her.

The problem was that the fears did not go away. Millie had spent her whole life waking up terrified that something awful would happen. She feared for her children. She feared for her husband. Most of all, Millie was terrified that perhaps she wasn't truly a Christian. She was terrified that Jesus would say that she had no faith and that he would reject her.

When Millie first read the armor of God material, the first 4 weapons discouraged her. None of those weapons seemed strong enough to free Millie from her paralysis.

When she read the story of the helmet, she began to have hope for the first time in her life. When she read about how obsessive thoughts jackhammer our brains and laugh at us in our helplessness, she felt someone finally understood her. When she read about how it is foolish to tell your mind to stop thinking something, she actually shouted out loud. At the same time, she began to cry. Soon the cries became sobs. Maybe there was hope for her. Maybe she hadn't failed God totally.

That was over 12 years ago. Millie now has 15 chapters of God's word that she quotes every week. She no longer tries to answer the fears. She simply fills her mind with God's powerful word. She still has a fearful thought every now and then. When she does, Millie just smiles and spends extra time quoting God's Word out loud.

Millie is one of the most joyful, confident, lighthearted women you will ever meet. You would never guess that Millie used to be ruled by fear. Millie is a living testimony of the power of God's word.

Prayers answered immediately

Quoting God's word brings about the most immediate of all answered prayers. Maybe that is why I am addicted to this power.

Ready to go on the offensive

The first 5 pieces of armor give us a very healthy, humble soul, filled with the heart of God. We are now ready for the sword. The sword is the most powerful attack weapon in the armor.

God's Voice
=
Sword

13

Hearing
God's Voice

...and the sword of the Spirit which is the word of God Ephesians 6:17

By the time I get to the sixth piece of the armor, I am overflowing with God's heart through me.

When I take up the Sword of the Spirit, I ask God to give me faith to hear his voice today. I realize that God's voice may come to me through:

> ➤ a scripture,
> ➤ an impression, or
> ➤ a circumstance.

I am relaxed. My main goal is to declare that I am available for him to lead me this day.

For those who are led by the Spirit of God are the children of God.
Romans 8:14

This sword is not the "logos" of God but the "rhema" of God.

You may already be familiar with the important distinction between these 2 words since it is commonly taught across the country. "*Logos*" and "*rhema*" are 2 Greek words that are both translated "*word*," but they are 2 very different words.

"*Logos*" denotes the expression of thought as embodied in an idea, a saying, a discourse, or a title. The emphasis of "*logos*" is that it denotes an already established word. The "*logos*" of God, therefore, usually refers to the written scriptures.

"*Rhema*" denotes that which is spoken or uttered. *Rhema* comes from the root word "*rheo,*" which means "*to flow.*" The emphasis of *rhema* is that it is always present tense. Ephesians 6:17 uses the word "*Rhema.*"

Extreme overreactions to hearing God's voice

One extreme overreaction is to deny that a Christian can hear God's voice. Four times in John 10, Jesus said that the mark of a Christian is that they hear his voice.

> *The man who enters by the gate is the shepherd of his sheep.*
> *The watchman opens the gate for him, and the*
> **sheep listen to his voice.**
> *He calls his own sheep by name and leads them out. When he has brought out all his own, he goes on ahead of them, and his sheep follow him because*
> **they know his voice.**
> *But they will never follow a stranger; in fact, they will run away from him because they do not recognize a stranger's voice.* [16] *I have other sheep that are not of this sheep pen. I must bring them also.*
> **They too will listen to my voice,**
> *and there shall be one flock and one shepherd.* [27]
> **My sheep listen to my voice;**
> *I know them, and they follow me. John 10:2-5, 16, 27*

Hebrews tells us to be careful to listen to God's voice.

See to it that
you do not refuse him who speaks.
If they did not escape when they refused him who warned them on earth, how much less will we, if we turn away from him who warns us from Heaven?
Hebrews 12:25

Today, *if you* **hear his voice,**
do not harden your hearts. Hebrews 3:7-8, 15, 4:7

The other extreme overreaction is for Christians to give too much weight to their guesses of what they think God is saying to them.

Scripture is clear that our hearing God's voice is often a vague guess. We have to hold our impressions fairly lightly and always submit these impressions to God's written word.

For we know in part and we prophesy in part I Corinthians 13:9

For now we see through a glass, darkly I Corinthians 13:12 (KJV)

I am open to your direction today.

When I pray on the sixth piece of armor, I simply declare that my heart is open to hear his specific direction for me in anything this day. In some ways, the Sword of the Spirit is another declaration of Jesus' lordship in my life.

If I ever sense a circumstance, scripture, or an impression that makes me think that Jesus is guiding me in a specific direction, I use 3 tests.

1. Is it Biblical?
2. Would people of godly wisdom see this as the direction of Jesus?
3. Does it cause me to bear more long-term fruit for Jesus?

God wants to speak to us. The sixth piece of armor reminds us to listen for his voice.

Roger

Roger loves Jesus. He has prayed on God's armor for many years, and he has had many times when he sensed that Jesus was speaking to him or guiding him.

Roger's favorite story is about his brother, Leon. Leon was not a Christian, and Roger had prayed for him for many years. Whenever Roger took up the Shield of Faith, he would say aloud, "Jesus, I trust you to bring Leon to you."

Roger reads his Bible every day while eating breakfast. Then he takes a 30 minute walk and prays on the armor during his lunch break.

One morning, Roger was reading in the book of Acts when a specific verse seemed to jump off of the page.

*So the church throughout all Judea and Galilee and Samaria enjoyed peace, being built up; and going on in the **fear** of the **Lord** and in the **comfort** of the **Holy Spirit**, it continued to increase. Acts 9:31 (NAS)*

Roger was struck by the fact that the disciples had the fear of the Lord and the comfort of the Holy Spirit. That day at lunch, as he prayed for Leon, he again remembered that verse. When he took up the Sword of the Spirit, he felt a nudge from the Holy Spirit. The Holy Spirit seemed to be telling him to pray this verse over his brother Leon. All that day, he kept praying this verse over his brother. That night as he went to sleep, he felt a peace that he had finished what the Lord wanted him to do. About 2 in the morning he was awakened by a phone call. It was his brother calling from the hospital to say that he'd been in a bad accident.

When Roger got to the hospital, Leon told him about how his car had hydroplaned. Leon said, "Rog, I was heading right toward a cliff. I was terrified. I felt like I was going to die, and I knew that I would be in hell forever. At the same time, though, I felt like God was holding me. It is a miracle that I didn't die. Rog, I am ready to become a Christian. Will you please forgive your stubborn old brother for resisting you and Jesus for so long?"

Roger was stunned. Jesus had given the fear of the Lord and the comfort of the Holy Spirit to his brother, just like he had prayed.

There were many tears of joy that night, and the angels in Heaven rejoiced.

Roger has had many times when he sensed that Jesus was speaking to him. This story, however, will always be his favorite.

Prayers answered immediately

The immediate response to this prayer is a sweet sense of trust. I don't have to hear anything right away. I am resting in the confidence that I have set my heart to hear my Lord. I am open and submissive to his voice and his direction in my life

Ready

=

Pray in the Spirit on all occasions

14

Ready

"And pray in the Spirit on all occasions with all kinds of prayers and requests.
With this in mind, be alert and always keep on praying for all the saints."
Ephesians 6:18

This seventh piece of armor launches us into the rest of our day!

After 6 clearly defined pieces of God's armor, Paul changes the focus on the seventh piece of armor. Rather than specific subjects, Paul now encourages a flexible alertness in prayer for the rest of the day.

I have written very little on this seventh piece of armor since Paul's goal was for each of us to develop our own flexible style in praying all day. When I pray on this seventh piece of armor, I ask God to make me aware of his presence and ready to fulfill his purposes all day long.

This works! I find the results of this seventh piece of armor to be very effective. I find my mind alert. I have many instances when a prayer flows out of my mouth later in the day as automatically as breathing.

The seventh piece of armor is often only a one sentence prayer, but it lasts all day.

> ➤ I may feel a song of worship flowing out of my heart later in the day.

> ➤ I may have someone share a need with me, and I immediately ask them if I can pray a short prayer for them right then.

> ➤ I have had times of re-praying on the entire armor.

> ➤ I may have a hunger to read more of God's word as I am going to sleep.

> ➤ I may have a situation arise during the day when I find myself asking the Lord for more wisdom and peace in my schedule (shoes) or more favor in my life (shield).

> ➤ The most common result is that I find myself breathing single sentence prayers all day long.

I use this seventh weapon to launch me into a love-dialogue with my king all day long.

We rest, trusting that he will stir us when he wants us to pray about anything throughout our day. Peace and joy immediately fill our hearts.

How to Get Started

15

Take
the
10 Day Test

Become an astronaut

Reading this book is like reading about the space shuttle. Doing the 10 day test is similar to the experience of flying the shuttle into space.

In one case, you have knowledge. In the other case, you have a life-changing experience. In this 10 day test, you will experience something much more powerful than flying a space shuttle.

It has been my joy to share this armor of God material with my church family every year since 1994. I have seen thousands of people's lives filled with power every day through God's armor.

However, I have also seen many people who get overwhelmed with all of this information, and they get stuck. They don't know how to get started. That is why this last section may be the most important part of the book.

As you prepare to launch into space, please re-watch the 7 short videos. They will energize you as you start praying.

During the 10 day test I ask you to:

➢ Use the prayer sheet to pray on God's armor, out loud and faithfully, every day for 7 days.

➢ Then have 3 days where you do not pray on God's armor. You are welcome to pray any other prayers on those 3 days, but don't pray on the armor.

Please follow these 5 starter tips carefully.

1. <u>Use the prayer sheet.</u>

   The end of this chapter contains extra copies of the one-page prayer sheet. This allows you to tear one out to take with you. The prayer sheet gives a brief overview of how to pray on all 7 pieces of armor.

2. <u>Have a specific time or activity dedicated to praying on God's armor.</u>

   If you already have a consistent, dedicated prayer time of at least 30 minutes, then you can use that time.

   If you do not have that consistent, dedicated time, then please consider using your drive time. You can turn off the radio and commune with Jesus on your commute.

   Another option is to take a 30 minute walk every day.

3. <u>Pray aloud.</u>

   It is with your mouth that you confess and are saved. Romans 10:10

   It is written, I believed, therefore I have spoken. With that same Spirit of faith, we also believe and therefore speak. II Corinthians 4:13

   Praying aloud releases faith, keeps you alert, and gives you much more power. We don't really know what is on our heart until we hear what comes out of our mouth in prayer.

4.   Listen to the Holy Spirit with each piece of armor.

The Holy Spirit searches our hearts. Romans 8:26-27

It is exciting to sense his leading. You will have a clear sense of this leading when you are done with each piece of armor. You will begin to get to know the Holy Spirit as the one who helps you put on each piece of armor, much like the armor bearer helps a warrior put on his armor.

"But the Helper, the Holy Spirit,
whom the Father will send in My name, He will teach you all things, and
bring to your remembrance all that I said to you. John 14:26 (NAS)

5.   Start on a Wednesday

Wednesday seems to be the best day to start. Your 7 days of praying on the armor will be Wednesday through Tuesday. Then your 3 days of praying any other way, except praying on the armor, will be the following Wednesday through Friday.

When you see the dramatic difference between the first 7 days and the last 3 days, I'm confident you'll want to pray on God's armor for the rest of your life

You will be stronger every month.

God's armor makes a dramatic and immediate difference in your day. God's armor also grows bigger in your heart every year.

It took me more than 5 years of daily prayer for the Belt of Truth to fit comfortably, and it took 10 years for the Breastplate of Righteousness to fit perfectly.

Many days I did not finish praying the entire armor. Yet, every month, I grew stronger in Jesus.

As you grow in the truth of each piece of armor, you will see more and more of God's power as a daily part of your life. I pray that the power of God's armor will make you strong in Jesus.

16

Removable Prayer Sheets

The following pages contain 5 copies removable Prayer Sheet for your convenience.

Feel free to cut out a page and place it in your areas of prayer.

An 8.5 x 11 printer ready version can be downloaded at www.prayersansweredimmediately.org under the free-resources tab.

Start

1. **I enter God's Most Holy Place** by the blood of Jesus to receive mercy and find grace. *Hebrews 4:16*

2. **I welcome you, Holy Spirit,** and ask you to make me strong in God's armor. *Romans 8:26-27*

Conflicts - Belt

1. **I drink of the Spirit of Truth. John 16:13**
   - ➤ I invite you to search my heart Spirit of Truth and give me truth in the innermost part of my being. *Psalm 51:6*
   - ➤ May my legacy (the fruit of my loins) I leave in my children and my ministry bear the fruit of truth. *Ephesians 6:14*

2. **I claim truth to avoid tensions. John 14:6**
   - ➤ Humility – By Jesus' love, I ask for a desire to hear Jesus' heart through others, through the listening test. *Isaiah 66:2*
   - ➤ Security – I claim grace to be calmly honest in gracious ways that help us all to find Jesus' heart. *Ephesians 4:15, 4:25-27*

Emotions - Breastplate

1. **I receive my Father's pleasure.**
   Spirit of Sonship, please place within me and fill me with my Father's pleasure, acceptance, and approval of me because I am lost to self and found in Jesus. (Keep drinking until filled) *Romans 8:15, 15:7, Isaiah 32:17, Philippians 1:12, 3:9, Psalm 16:3, Proverbs 3:12, Ephesians 1:5, II Timothy 2:15*

2. **I receive power over sin.**
   I claim open eyes to see life and death, and I claim your nature and strength through me to walk in life. (Pray over specific sin patterns) *Romans 7:11-13, 8:1-6*

3. **I claim freedom from trying to please, from criticizing or from being criticized. I receive a loving heart to bless others.** (Keep drinking until filled) *Romans 8:14*

Schedule - Shoes

1. **"Counselor" please show me wisdom** &

2. **"Comforter" please show me peace in:**
   - ➤ My schedule today
   - ➤ My evening
   - ➤ The direction of my life
   - ➤ My eating and exercise habits
     John 14:16 and 26, 15:26, 16:7

Favor - Shield

1. **Spirit of Faith I drink deeply today of faith.**
   II Corinthians 4:13
   - ➤ I receive the gift of faith. *Ephesians 2:8*
   - ➤ I take up the Shield of Faith today to extinguish all the flaming arrows of Satan. *Ephesians 6:16*

2. **I trust you to…, I receive…, I claim…**

Thoughts - Helmet

1. **I claim eternal life in Jesus this day.**
   I John 5:13, 1 Timothy 3:13, 2 Peter 1:10-11

2. **I claim Heaven's perspective and the mind of Christ.**
   I Corinthians 2:16

3. **I claim a hunger to memorize your word.** *Psalm 119:11*

God's voice - Sword

I claim that I am your sheep today, and I will hear your voice and trust you to lead me. *John 10, Romans 8:14*

Ready - Pray in the Spirit on all occasions with all kinds of prayers and requests.

I trust you, Holy Spirit to pray through me all day long.

Start

1. **I enter God's Most Holy Place** by the blood of Jesus to receive mercy and find grace. *Hebrews 4:16*

2. **I welcome you, Holy Spirit,** and ask you to make me strong in God's armor. *Romans 8:26-27*

Conflicts - Belt

1. **I drink of the Spirit of Truth. John 16:13**
   - ➤ I invite you to search my heart Spirit of Truth and give me truth in the innermost part of my being. *Psalm 51:6*
   - ➤ May my legacy (the fruit of my loins) I leave in my children and my ministry bear the fruit of truth. *Ephesians 6:14*

2. **I claim truth to avoid tensions. John 14:6**
   - ➤ Humility – By Jesus' love, I ask for a desire to hear Jesus' heart through others, through the listening test. *Isaiah 66:2*
   - ➤ Security – I claim grace to be calmly honest in gracious ways that help us all to find Jesus' heart. *Ephesians 4:15, 4:25-27*

Emotions - Breastplate

1. **I receive my Father's pleasure.**
   Spirit of Sonship, please place within me and fill me with my Father's pleasure, acceptance, and approval of me because I am lost to self and found in Jesus. (Keep drinking until filled) *Romans 8:15, 15:7, Isaiah 32:17, Philippians 1:12, 3:9, Psalm 16:3, Proverbs 3:12, Ephesians 1:5, II Timothy 2:15*

2. **I receive power over sin.**
   I claim open eyes to see life and death, and I claim your nature and strength through me to walk in life. (Pray over specific sin patterns) *Romans 7:11-13, 8:1-6*

3. **I claim freedom from trying to please, from criticizing or from being criticized. I receive a loving heart to bless others.** (Keep drinking until filled) *Romans 8:14*

Schedule - Shoes

1. **"Counselor" please show me wisdom** &

2. **"Comforter" please show me peace in:**
   - ➢ My schedule today
   - ➢ My evening
   - ➢ The direction of my life
   - ➢ My eating and exercise habits
     John 14:16 and 26, 15:26, 16:7

Favor - Shield

1. **Spirit of Faith I drink deeply today of faith.**
   II Corinthians 4:13
   - ➢ I receive the gift of faith. *Ephesians 2:8*
   - ➢ I take up the Shield of Faith today to extinguish all the flaming arrows of Satan. *Ephesians 6:16*

2. **I trust you to..., I receive..., I claim...**

Thoughts - Helmet

1. **I claim eternal life in Jesus this day.**
   I John 5:13, 1 Timothy 3:13, 2 Peter 1:10-11

2. **I claim Heaven's perspective and the mind of Christ.**
   I Corinthians 2:16

3. **I claim a hunger to memorize your word.** *Psalm 119:11*

God's voice - Sword

I claim that I am your sheep today, and I will hear your voice and trust you to lead me. *John 10, Romans 8:14*

Ready - Pray in the Spirit on all occasions with all kinds of prayers and requests.

I trust you, Holy Spirit to pray through me all day long.

Start

1. **I enter God's Most Holy Place** by the blood of Jesus to receive mercy and find grace. *Hebrews 4:16*

2. **I welcome you, Holy Spirit,** and ask you to make me strong in God's armor. *Romans 8:26-27*

Conflicts - Belt

1. **I drink of the Spirit of Truth. John 16:13**
   - ➤ I invite you to search my heart Spirit of Truth and give me truth in the innermost part of my being. *Psalm 51:6*
   - ➤ May my legacy (the fruit of my loins) I leave in my children and my ministry bear the fruit of truth. *Ephesians 6:14*

2. **I claim truth to avoid tensions. John 14:6**
   - ➤ Humility – By Jesus' love, I ask for a desire to hear Jesus' heart through others, through the listening test. *Isaiah 66:2*
   - ➤ Security – I claim grace to be calmly honest in gracious ways that help us all to find Jesus' heart. *Ephesians 4:15, 4:25-27*

Emotions - Breastplate

1. **I receive my Father's pleasure.**
   Spirit of Sonship, please place within me and fill me with my Father's pleasure, acceptance, and approval of me because I am lost to self and found in Jesus. (Keep drinking until filled) *Romans 8:15, 15:7, Isaiah 32:17, Philippians 1:12, 3:9, Psalm 16:3, Proverbs 3:12, Ephesians 1:5, II Timothy 2:15*

2. **I receive power over sin.**
   I claim open eyes to see life and death, and I claim your nature and strength through me to walk in life. (Pray over specific sin patterns) *Romans 7:11-13, 8:1-6*

3. **I claim freedom from trying to please, from criticizing or from being criticized. I receive a loving heart to bless others.** (Keep drinking until filled) *Romans 8:14*

Schedule - Shoes

1. <u>**"Counselor" please show me wisdom**</u> &
 	
   2. <u>**"Comforter" please show me peace in:**</u>
     ➢ My schedule today
     ➢ My evening
     ➢ The direction of my life
     ➢ My eating and exercise habits
            John 14:16 and 26, 15:26, 16:7

Favor - Shield

1. <u>**Spirit of Faith I drink deeply today of faith.**</u>
     II Corinthians 4:13
     ➢ I receive the gift of faith. *Ephesians 2:8*
     ➢ I take up the Shield of Faith today to extinguish all the flaming arrows of Satan. *Ephesians 6:16*
 	
   2. <u>**I trust you to…, I receive…, I claim…**</u>

Thoughts - Helmet

1. <u>**I claim eternal life in Jesus this day.**</u>
     I John 5:13, 1 Timothy 3:13, 2 Peter 1:10-11
 	
   2. <u>**I claim Heaven's perspective and the mind of Christ.**</u>
     I Corinthians 2:16
 	
   3. <u>**I claim a hunger to memorize your word.**</u> *Psalm 119:11*

God's voice - Sword
I claim that I am your sheep today, and I will hear your voice and trust you to lead me. *John 10, Romans 8:14*
Ready - Pray in the Spirit on all occasions with all kinds of prayers and requests.
I trust you, Holy Spirit to pray through me all day long.

Start

1. **I enter God's Most Holy Place** by the blood of Jesus to receive mercy and find grace. *Hebrews 4:16*

2. **I welcome you, Holy Spirit,** and ask you to make me strong in God's armor. *Romans 8:26-27*

Conflicts - Belt

1. **I drink of the Spirit of Truth. John 16:13**
    - ➤ I invite you to search my heart Spirit of Truth and give me truth in the innermost part of my being. *Psalm 51:6*
    - ➤ May my legacy (the fruit of my loins) I leave in my children and my ministry bear the fruit of truth. *Ephesians 6:14*

2. **I claim truth to avoid tensions. John 14:6**
    - ➤ Humility – By Jesus' love, I ask for a desire to hear Jesus' heart through others, through the listening test. *Isaiah 66:2*
    - ➤ Security – I claim grace to be calmly honest in gracious ways that help us all to find Jesus' heart. *Ephesians 4:15, 4:25-27*

Emotions - Breastplate

1. **I receive my Father's pleasure.**
    Spirit of Sonship, please place within me and fill me with my Father's pleasure, acceptance, and approval of me because I am lost to self and found in Jesus. (Keep drinking until filled) *Romans 8:15, 15:7, Isaiah 32:17, Philippians 1:12, 3:9, Psalm 16:3, Proverbs 3:12, Ephesians 1:5, II Timothy 2:15*

2. **I receive power over sin.**
    I claim open eyes to see life and death, and I claim your nature and strength through me to walk in life. (Pray over specific sin patterns) *Romans 7:11-13, 8:1-6*

3. **I claim freedom from trying to please, from criticizing or from being criticized. I receive a loving heart to bless others.** (Keep drinking until filled) *Romans 8:14*

Schedule - Shoes

1. <u>**"Counselor" please show me wisdom**</u> &

2. <u>**"Comforter" please show me peace in:**</u>
   - ➤ My schedule today
   - ➤ My evening
   - ➤ The direction of my life
   - ➤ My eating and exercise habits
     John 14:16 and 26, 15:26, 16:7

Favor - Shield

1. <u>**Spirit of Faith I drink deeply today of faith.**</u>
   II Corinthians 4:13
   - ➤ I receive the gift of faith. *Ephesians 2:8*
   - ➤ I take up the Shield of Faith today to extinguish all the flaming arrows of Satan. *Ephesians 6:16*

2. <u>**I trust you to…, I receive…, I claim…**</u>

Thoughts - Helmet

1. <u>**I claim eternal life in Jesus this day.**</u>
   I John 5:13, 1 Timothy 3:13, 2 Peter 1:10-11

2. <u>**I claim Heaven's perspective and the mind of Christ.**</u>
   I Corinthians 2:16

3. <u>**I claim a hunger to memorize your word.**</u> *Psalm 119:11*

God's voice - Sword

I claim that I am your sheep today, and I will hear your voice and trust you to lead me. *John 10, Romans 8:14*

Ready - Pray in the Spirit on all occasions with all kinds of prayers and requests.

I trust you, Holy Spirit to pray through me all day long.

Start

1. **I enter God's Most Holy Place** by the blood of Jesus to receive mercy and find grace. *Hebrews 4:16*

2. **I welcome you, Holy Spirit,** and ask you to make me strong in God's armor. *Romans 8:26-27*

Conflicts - Belt

1. **I drink of the Spirit of Truth. John 16:13**
   - ➤ I invite you to search my heart Spirit of Truth and give me truth in the innermost part of my being. *Psalm 51:6*
   - ➤ May my legacy (the fruit of my loins) I leave in my children and my ministry bear the fruit of truth. *Ephesians 6:14*

2. **I claim truth to avoid tensions. John 14:6**
   - ➤ Humility – By Jesus' love, I ask for a desire to hear Jesus' heart through others, through the listening test. *Isaiah 66:2*
   - ➤ Security – I claim grace to be calmly honest in gracious ways that help us all to find Jesus' heart. *Ephesians 4:15, 4:25-27*

Emotions - Breastplate

1. **I receive my Father's pleasure.**
   Spirit of Sonship, please place within me and fill me with my Father's pleasure, acceptance, and approval of me because I am lost to self and found in Jesus. (Keep drinking until filled) *Romans 8:15, 15:7, Isaiah 32:17, Philippians 1:12, 3:9, Psalm 16:3, Proverbs 3:12, Ephesians 1:5, II Timothy 2:15*

2. **I receive power over sin.**
   I claim open eyes to see life and death, and I claim your nature and strength through me to walk in life. (Pray over specific sin patterns) *Romans 7:11-13, 8:1-6*

3. **I claim freedom from trying to please, from criticizing or from being criticized. I receive a loving heart to bless others.** (Keep drinking until filled) *Romans 8:14*

Schedule - Shoes

1. **<u>"Counselor" please show me wisdom</u>** &

2. **<u>"Comforter" please show me peace in:</u>**
    - ➤ My schedule today
    - ➤ My evening
    - ➤ The direction of my life
    - ➤ My eating and exercise habits
        John 14:16 and 26, 15:26, 16:7

Favor - Shield

1. **<u>Spirit of Faith I drink deeply today of faith.</u>**
    II Corinthians 4:13
    - ➤ I receive the gift of faith. *Ephesians 2:8*
    - ➤ I take up the Shield of Faith today to extinguish all the flaming arrows of Satan. *Ephesians 6:16*

2. **<u>I trust you to…, I receive…, I claim…</u>**

Thoughts - Helmet

1. **<u>I claim eternal life in Jesus this day.</u>**
    I John 5:13, 1 Timothy 3:13, 2 Peter 1:10-11

2. **<u>I claim Heaven's perspective and the mind of Christ.</u>**
    I Corinthians 2:16

3. **<u>I claim a hunger to memorize your word.</u>** *Psalm 119:11*

God's voice - Sword

I claim that I am your sheep today, and I will hear your voice and trust you to lead me. *John 10, Romans 8:14*

Ready - Pray in the Spirit on all occasions with all kinds of prayers and requests.

I trust you, Holy Spirit to pray through me all day long.

Appendices

Appendix A

Understanding God's Favor

The truth that guides my prayers when I pray on the Shield of Faith is a scriptural understanding of God's favor. Everyone comes into his walk with Christ with many preconceived notions. We form mental boxes growing up that we base solely on our experiences and not on God's word. These assumptions become our security.

Then, when we become Christians, we try to squeeze God into our little boxes. This is why an in-depth study of God's word is so important. The more deeply we study God's word, the more he can break open our boxes and teach us to approach subjects from his perspective.

One of my preconceived notions, or boxes, that I brought into Christianity was that I thought I needed to earn God's favor. I believed that every "specific blessing" that God poured into my life was a direct result of some "specific act of obedience" on my part. This was a "works mentality."

Like most people with boxes, there was some truth to my paradigm. Scripture speaks clearly about sowing and reaping. It also extols the blessings of obedience. Jesus taught on this theme of obedience throughout his final sermon in John 14 through 17. As a counselor, I find that godly character can often be specifically identified as a major reason for success in ministries, marriages, careers, families, finances, etc. Many times, specific blessings are a direct result of specific acts of obedience.

My error was that I took this truth to the extreme. I believed that "every" blessing was a direct result of some act of obedience. I became a slave to a cause and effect mentality.

Taken to the extreme, this doctrine leads us to believe that if we want to be blessed by God, we must always perform some specific act of obedience, and then God will pour out that specific blessing.

An in-depth study of scripture on this point is eye-opening. As we study the lives of Abraham, Isaac, Jacob, Moses, Joshua, and David, we get a view of God's favor from an entirely different perspective. We find that God's favor is like a mantle that God places on our lives. When we have this mantle, it produces amazing results.

Good gifts come to us because we ask.

Scripture is clear that obedience is a major factor in God's blessing.

My shock was in discovering that, just as big of a factor as obedience in these men's lives, was simply that they asked God to bless them.

The word of God teaches 2 astounding truths:

1. God likes for us to ask him to bless us.

> *Jabez cried out to the God of Israel, "Oh that you would bless me and*
> *enlarge my territory! Let your hand be with me and keep me from*
> *harm so that I will be free from pain." And God granted his request.*
> *1 Chronicles 4:10*

2. The favor or blessing of God means that good things
    that happen to us cannot be traced to any specific act
    of obedience.

    In other words, God blesses you just because you
    ask. The scriptural examples of this truth are so
    numerous that they are overwhelming: Abraham in
    Egypt, Jacob stealing the blessing, David not dying
    from his sin with Bathsheba, etc. Learn to look for 2
    phrases in the Bible. Wherever it says, *"the Lord was
    with him"* or *"the Lord gave him success in everything he
    did,"* that means the favor of God on his life went
    beyond cause and effect!

Recognizing this truth changed my prayer life. Now there
are 2 reasons why I am confident that our church will stay
healthy, my marriage will be strong, my kids will be godly,
and my finances will be sound. The first reason I'm
confident in these areas is because I am determined to walk
in obedience to God in all these areas. The second reason is
because I regularly take up my Shield of Faith and speak out
loud that I trust God to give me his favor to cover these
areas.

Honesty versus faith

Let's cut to the chase. Let's get to the bottom-line issue of
how to sense God's presence when we pray. Over 90
percent of all the recorded prayers in the Bible are found in
the book of Psalms. From the Psalms, we learn that Biblical
prayers always begin with honesty. Prayer doesn't begin
until we acknowledge the problem:

I am angry./ I am hurting./ I have sinned./ I have strayed./
I am confused./ I am being attacked./ I have been prideful./

I am lonely./ I feel distant from you./ I am frightened./ I
am tempted./ I am impatient.

Beginning with honesty is obviously the logical, Biblical
pattern for starting our prayers.

Here is an extremely important question. How do we feel
after we have been honest in our prayers?

Let's pick one or 2 examples from that list of 12 examples of
honest prayer. Let's pick "angry" and "lonely." If we got
honest in prayer and gave full vent to the strength of our
anger or our loneliness, how would we feel afterwards?

Would we feel better or worse?

We would feel worse! In fact, we might feel absolutely lousy!
As necessary as honesty is in prayer, it does not make us feel
better. A deep, transparent acknowledging of the problem
usually makes us feel miserable.

This misunderstanding causes many people to avoid prayer.
This affects men more often than women.

Men are focused on productivity. In Genesis 3, when God
cursed Adam, he cursed his productivity. When God cursed
Eve, he cursed her relationships.

Men instinctively know that if they open up and are honest
about what's inside their hearts, they will feel worse instead
of better.

From a man's perspective, "If prayer just makes me feel
worse, then prayer is not very productive."

That is why, in nearly every Psalm, there is a turning point
where the psalmist begins to say out loud:

> ➢   I trust you to rescue me.

> ➢ I trust you to guide me.

> ➢ I trust you to protect me.

> ➢ I trust you to convict me.

> ➢ I trust you to draw me to you.

Faith releases the presence of God in our lives.

I have 2 simple questions for people who have a hard time sensing God's presence when praying.

1. What percentage of your thoughts and prayers are spent dwelling on the problem?

2. What percentage of your thoughts and prayers are spent pouring faith through your heart and mouth into trusting God to solve the situation?

If we have a hard time sensing God's presence when praying, it's likely that we spend too much of our time and energy brooding on the problem?

Again, I'd like to repeat that honestly acknowledging the problem is a necessary beginning to prayer. It is often a legitimate way to sift our hearts, to identify what things are really bothering us, to groan in intercession, or to get direction from the Lord.

To be powerful in prayer, though, the major portion of our prayer lives and the conclusion of all of our prayers must be to cover our problems with faith.

Faith is the currency of Heaven.

Appendix B

How to Memorize
Chapters of God's Word

I have hidden your word in my heart that I might not sin against you.
Psalm 119:11

Hunger-based memorization

I love salmon.

If you made me eat 5 pounds of salmon in 5 minutes every day, however, I would grow to hate the taste of salmon.

Memorizing chapters is meat to our souls. People kill their love of memorizing by shoving 5 pounds of meat down their own throats in 5 minutes.

They could have gone 10 times slower and had 30 chapters of God's word memorized 30 years later. Because they rushed, 30 years later they don't even have 30 verses, much less 30 chapters, memorized.

When I think that I am ready to move on to another verse, I always make myself wait 3 to 7 more days. By the time I finally get to tackle the new verse, I am ravenously hungry to memorize this verse.

Pick a chapter where you love every single verse.

Memorizing a 16 verse chapter is like adopting 16 children. You will spend weeks getting to know each verse. Each verse will become one of your children.

If you pick a chapter that has 4 great verses and 12 average verses, you will become bored and lose the inspiration. You won't want to adopt any more children. Please pick a chapter where each verse is precious and beautiful. Of my memory chapters, I have 15 chapters that I recommend to people to choose as a possible first chapter. These 15 chapters are extremely inspiring in every verse.

Psalm 19	Psalm 149
Psalm 23	Isaiah 53
Psalm 84	Isaiah 61
Psalm 91	John 14
Psalm 103	Romans 12
Psalm 121	1 Corinthians 13
Psalm 131	Revelation 19
Psalm 133	

My other memory chapters are:

Psalm 111, Proverbs 3, Isaiah 55, Matthew 18, John 15, Romans 6 & 8, II Corinthians 1-7, Ephesians 1 & 2, Philippians 1-4, Colossians 3, II Timothy 2-4, Hebrews 12, James 1, and II Peter 1.

Adopt each verse like a child.

Because I spend weeks learning an individual verse, I take the time to get to know the verse. I play games with each verse.

- ➤ I count the words in each verse and make up musical rhythms by breaking the verse down into 2, 3, and 4 word counts.

- ➤ I will often sing the verses and make them into songs.

- ➤ I look for alliteration in the key words.

- ➤ I take the first letter in certain key words and create acronyms.

- ➤ I chew on the content until I have written 3 to 5 notes of insight from that verse into my Bible. I want to know every detail of that verse.

For example, II Timothy 4:13 starts off with the 3 words, "*When you come*".

> *When you come, bring the cloak that I left with Carpus at Troas, and my scrolls, especially the parchments. II Timothy 4:13*

I used the verse number, 4:13, to remind me that the verse begins with a key, 3 word phrase.

Also, I connected the word *"cloak"* and *"Carpus,"* 2 words that begin with a "C," to form an alliterative reminder.

There are many emotional insights in II Timothy 4:13. The fact that Paul was asking for his cloak meant that he was probably cold in a dark, damp dungeon. It is possible that his scrolls are his correspondence, but his parchments are his copies of God's Word. I wondered what type of person Carpus was. I was touched by how sure Paul was that Timothy would come.

I find buried emotion and rich truths in every verse.

Get excited when you can't remember a part of a verse.

Even after quoting a chapter hundreds of times over a decade, I can have a brain burp where I cannot immediately remember a certain part of a verse.

At that time, I get very excited. I know that Jesus is going to give me a new insight into the part of the verse that I cannot remember.

Appendix C

An Offer to Pastors

Books for every member of your church

100% of the profits from this book are dedicated to letting pastors know about this book and giving this book away for free to pastors who will teach this material to their church in a sermon series.

If a pastor is willing to pray on the armor daily in his own life and to teach the prayer weapons as a sermon series, then we will supply that pastor with enough copies of this book for every member and visitor to have their own copy.

I have been a pastor for over 3 decades. It is a great honor to encourage and serve other pastors. Pastors have the hardest job and the best job in the world. I love them so much. They are my heroes.

An explosion of visitors and church growth

The pastor could use this series as an effective outreach.

1. The pastor orders the books so that they arrive 3 months before the scheduled teaching series.

2. The pastor orders thousands of full color, high gloss business cards that arrive at the same time as the books. 5,000 graphically designed, glossy, full-color business cards cost approximately $100.

    The front of the cards would have the following basic information arranged in an attractive format.

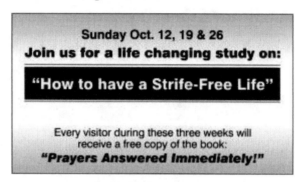

    The back of the card would usually have a map to the church, the website, address, service times, and phone number. (The series may go longer than 3 weeks, but you only want to list the first 3 weeks on the card.)

3. For 2 months, the pastor rallies his people, through testimonies and announcements, to read the book and to watch the free YouTube videos.

4. The last few weeks, the pastor challenges every member to give out 20 cards and to bring 2 to 5 visitors to this series. The best part is that the visitors will remain for the entire series. The card is engaging and attractive. Enthusiasm to invite guests comes from members whose lives have been changed through the book and the 10 day test. The free book is the final hook.

5. During the series, there would be testimonies that would open with the words: *"When I took the 10 day test…"* This guides the visitors to do more than just read the book.

An explosion of prayer

We become pastors because we yearn to help people connect with the living God.

> ➤ When our members are passionately in love with Jesus, they are faithful and a joy to pastor.

> ➤ However, when members lose their first love passion for Jesus, we feel them drifting away. Attendance becomes spotty. Petty issues distract them.

In a gaming, texting, social networking world, helping our people to have intimate, personal, daily time with Jesus is the cornerstone of our hopes for pastoral success.

The combination of the pastor's series, free books, free YouTube videos, personal testimonies, and small group discussions will lead most of your members to take the 10 day test.

Once your people take the 10 day test, you will have an explosion of prayer that will not be temporary. It will grow stronger every year.

Healthy Souls

The daily soaking of these prayers causes a gentle, consistent increase in soul health that continues for decades. People who daily pray on the armor of God grow into mature, cheerful, giving, and strife-free servants in their church family.

Because the truths of the armor grow stronger through daily prayer, people get healthier every year.

I have seen this fruit in my own church, and I yearn for others to experience this power.

Spread the Word!

Our vision is for millions of prayer lives to be permanently changed over the next 30 years. If you ask your people to link the YouTube videos to their social media, and they ask all of their friends to link the videos, that will spread the word.

Also, please tell every pastor you know about this offer and how it has impacted your church.

Pastors testing the book on a small scale first

Many pastors take a season and go through the book and videos with their staff or elders as a point of research. Other churches pick a few small groups and ask them to go through the book and videos. These options allow the pastor to investigate the results of this book on a smaller scale before leading the entire church in a study of the book.

Ordering books

If a pastor contacts us with a desire to teach this material as a sermon series, we will supply enough books for every member of the congregation to have a free book, if we have the funds available.

If we do not have the funds available, we will offer a pastor 2 options.

1. We can sell the books at our cost.

2. We can put this pastor on a waiting list with an estimate of how soon we would be able to have the free books available.

You can order the books through:

www.PrayersAnsweredImmediately.org